(Flo)

Best wishes and God bless!

Lee Updike

2010

HIS TOUCH

Spiritual Reality In Everyday Life

LEE UPDIKE

INFINITY
PUBLISHING

Copyright © 2010 by Lee Updike

ISBN 0-7414-5789-X

Scripture quotations from New King James Version
© Thomas Nelson, Inc.

Published by:

INFINITY
PUBLISHING
1094 New DeHaven Street, Suite 100
West Conshohocken, PA 19428-2713
Info@buybooksontheweb.com
www.buybooksontheweb.com
Toll-free (877) BUY BOOK
Local Phone (610) 941-9999
Fax (610) 941-9959

Printed in the United States of America
Publishe July 2010

DEDICATION

This book is dedicated to
a group of very special people,
my grandchildren

Timothy, Rachelle, Gordon,
Kenny, Andy, Meghan,
Dylan and Joey

ACKNOWLEDGMENTS

Few of these people participated in the creation of this book.
Each one however, contributed in some way
to my spiritual life.

My parents, Ryburn and Mary Updike,
sister, Jean and brothers, Harley and Dale.
My wife, Beverly, daughter, Janet
and sons, Daniel and Larry.

Klaus Peters, Dann Filyer, Jim Sleeth, Don Egan,
John and Doris Verdoold, Gerald Morgan, Roy Davis,
Don and Jean Weeks, Sam and Vivian Learning,
Carson Latimer, Otto Janzen, Robert Donnelly,
Lawrence Abrahamson, Howard and Audrey Rosassen,
Gary Ziehl, Gordon and Mary Campbell, Dan Baker,
Ches and Kathy Jacobs, Murray Coughlan, Dennis Walker,
Ron Steinbrenner, Adam Howorko, John Klamm,
George and Moyra Feller.

In recalling these special names, I soon realized they
should number in the hundreds. May the Lord's
blessing fall heavily on each one listed here, and
equally on the many others who should be.

FOREWORD

The book you hold in your hand will leave you with a desire to draw closer to God. My friend and parishioner, Lee Updike, gives an honest account of various events and stories that will build your faith and have you hungering for a deeper relationship with the Lord. As a Spirit-filled man of God, Lee has glorified his Master in highlighting His work through His Spirit. Both *"His Touch"* and Lee's previous book, *"Edge of the Wilderness"* are written in such a genuine and transparent manner that the reader soon feels as though they know the author.

The compilation of short stories makes for an easy read anywhere and any time. The author takes the reader from the supernatural workings of God to the natural experiences of a wilderness trapper, from the powerful conviction of the Holy Spirit in hardened hearts, to the ordinary activities of life, such as getting a shovel back from a neighbor. God's provision and protection are prominent throughout this book.

In these stories, one awakens to the fact that truly, the God who "knows the hairs of your head," is as concerned about the mundane affairs of your life as He is about the supremely important ones. The importance of a personal relationship with Christ, and the excitement of a Spirit-filled life are clearly presented. Any book that draws a person into the presence of God is definitely worth reading.

Rev. Dr. George I. Feller
Senior Pastor
Northwest Pentecostal Assembly

CONTENTS

CHAPTER 1

AN ENCOUNTER WITH JESUS

I was raised on a farm in northern Saskatchewan during the great depression of the 1930s and 40s. My parents were good people but spiritual things were hardly ever mentioned in our home. We never attended church. Before I was two, my dad was stricken with a chronic and debilitating illness. He was preoccupied with his own misfortune and often overwhelmed by pain; consequently, he had little time for me. His lack of involvement in my life caused an unintentional but troubling wound in my young spirit.

In my early twenties, I met and married a lovely young woman in Toronto, though both of us were too young and too immature for such a commitment. My young wife came from a dysfunctional home and had her share of inner problems, too. Our marriage was strife-ridden from the outset.

After ten years of frustration, we agreed to receive marriage counseling. The counselor was competent, the advice was sound but there was no power to make the changes we both needed. I even consulted a psychiatrist but found no answers. At 32, I was depressed and disillusioned with life. There seemed to be no help and no hope. My wife, Beverly and I made plans to separate. I had thoughts of suicide.

About that time, a random thought came to me from an unknown source. It dogged me persistently and I couldn't

1

get it out of my mind, "Why not try God?" Finally, I mentioned it to Bev. "You know we've never tried God in all our troubles," I ventured cautiously.

"Gotta go to church for that," she replied offhandedly.

"Oh," I said, already discouraged. I had attended formal churches several times as a young adult, but had sensed nothing real or compelling.

As it happened, the Baptists were hosting open-air services on Loblaw's parking lot that Sunday. For some reason we attended. Pastor Dann Filyer preached, and for the first time in my life, I heard the gospel of Jesus Christ. Pastor Dann spoke of a Christ who shed His blood and died on a wooden cross, and whom God had raised from the dead so that ordinary people, even very sinful ones, could have forgiveness for their sins, receive eternal life, and know the presence and the help of God to live this life.

We attended the outdoor services until they concluded about a month later. Then the Updike family began attending regular Sunday services in the beautiful new building the Baptist folk had erected near the heart of downtown Aurora. At the conclusion of each service, the Pastor issued an appeal to any who desired to receive Jesus Christ as Savior. I knew the message he preached was truth and I had hope that there was help in Jesus for me, too. However, I was just too hung-up to lift a hand or make any response to the altar calls.

At that time, I worked at General Electric in Toronto, 30 miles away. About two o-clock one morning in late September 1964, I was heading home after the late shift. As I rounded the off-ramp from the 401 onto Highway 400, north, out of the darkened sky came a steady, driving rain. As I drove and listened to the rhythm of the wipers and the whine of the tires on the wet pavement, I began to think about my life, my wife and two children, and Jesus. I desperately wanted to believe that all the things Pastor Dann preached could be true and real in my life, too, but I was afraid that somehow, after all, I would be excluded. While personal salvation was obviously a reality for many, I had no confidence that it could happen to me. I was very troubled.

I continued north on the 400. The twin headlight beams stabbed through the downpour and the darkness.

Suddenly, I was aware that someone was sitting beside me in the front seat! I don't know how I knew, but I knew, it was Him...Jesus! I trembled in awe and wonder; the power of His presence was overwhelming. I wept uncontrollably. I couldn't speak and He didn't. But, the kindness, forgiveness, and love in His gaze spoke into the depth of my soul. I knew it was real! I knew He was real! I knew He was alive, and despite a sure awareness that He knew everything there was to know about me, I had an inner certainty that he would never turn me away.

I, of course, didn't realize that I was seeing a vision, a glimpse into that 'other world,' made possible by the Holy Spirit. It is a rare and a holy privilege to receive such a communication from the Lord. Obviously He knew how strung-out I was, and what it would take to bring me to Himself.

Just as strangely and suddenly as He had come, He was gone, but His awesome presence lingered. For some reason I cried even harder. I had to pull over. In the distance, the headlights picked out the green highway sign for the King Road.

I sat there for a long time trying to compose myself, and trying to understand intellectually, what I had just experienced spiritually. I was not very successful, but one thing I was certain of, what had just happened was the most real and powerful experience of my entire life!

I felt that I should pray, a "sinner's prayer," as Pastor Dann called it. I didn't know how to go about it and in my ignorance, I thought that real prayer had to be prayed on your knees. (Not a bad idea, by the way) I decided to go home and pray there. I swung right onto the King Road, East. In twenty minutes, I was in my driveway at 1 Algonquin Crescent, in Aurora.

I entered the house quietly and went into the basement. Everyone was asleep as usual. I knelt on the concrete floor about two yards east of the furnace. I then stumbled through the most important prayer I've ever prayed. "Jesus," I cried, "You know that I don't really know how to pray. But tonight, there are several things I am now sure of. I know I'm a sinner. You died and Your blood was shed for so many, but tonight, I know You died for me, too. I know that you are alive, and Lord, whatever You can do for a man like me, please do it. Amen."

I didn't see or hear anything at that time, but a soft peace I'd never felt before crept over my inner being. It seemed like a great weight that I didn't even know was there, fell off my shoulders. I had an unexplainable sense that something that had never been right in my life was right at last. Although I did not understand, nor could I explain what had happened; nevertheless the effect of that encounter with Jesus was heart changing and life changing. The reality of it remains as vivid today as it was those 45-plus years ago.

Fortunately, I had the sense to realize that this spiritual experience, wonderful and deeply moving as it was, was just a beginning. How was I to get to know Jesus better, and how could I learn to properly live the new life He had given me? I had a great peace and joy in my heart but I couldn't imagine how I could become a mature Christian, like some of my new friends at the church. I soon found out...

We didn't have a Bible in our home. I had never felt it necessary to own one. However, just as mysteriously, as the thought, 'Why not try God' had come; now there came a relentless desire to read the Bible. The next day I went to Cole's in Newmarket and purchased one. I read it voraciously. I read it for hours at a time. Sometimes, after work in the early hours of the morning, I would begin reading and lose track of time. When the sun came up, I would still be reading. At times, I knew that what I was reading was so holy, that I had to get on my knees to read it.

I have had many wonderful encounters with Jesus over the years. He has guided and protected me. He has healed me, blessed me, and used me in miraculous ways, and I have deserved none of it. But it is God's way, the way of love, mercy and grace.

I am ashamed to confess that I have known serious failure in my Christian life. Nevertheless, I have discovered that, though he will correct swiftly and discipline appropriately, the same Christ who gave Himself for us when we were sinners, has love, grace and power to restore us, as broken Christians, too.

Some folks have said, "I'd like to be a Christian but I'm afraid I couldn't live the life." The truth is that none of us can live the life, except by the Spirit of Christ who lives in us and helps us continually. Moreover, if we fail, there can be restoration through the Lord Himself.

My wife surrendered herself to Christ, too, and received His mercy and His help. In time, the marriage that knew such stormy seas and near shipwreck sailed into peaceful waters.

It may be that you have not yet had a meeting with Jesus, or asked for His forgiveness, or invited Him to be the Lord of your life. I assure you He knows what you're facing in life, and He understands your heart perfectly, and He loves you with an unconditional love. He died as the sacrifice for your sins too. And He rose from the dead for this very thing...to help you in your deepest need, today, and for all of eternity.

What the Lord has done for me, He will do for you, and perhaps even more! He has no favorites. Your part is simply to surrender and believe. Jesus does the miracle part.

Today, I pass on to you the question that came to me and triggered the transformation of my life those years ago. The question is... "Why not try God?"

CHAPTER 2

THE CHALLENGE OF CHANGE

Certainly the Lord's optimum strategy by which we should come to Jesus and learn to walk in His ways would be that we should be born into a Christian home, be nurtured by godly parents and experience a loving, Christian environment through all our formative years.

Most of us, of course, have never known such a holy privilege. Personally, I was an accomplished sinner of 32 before I truly heard and responded to the gospel. While the miraculous nature of my conversion was wonderful, the day-by-day process of adjusting to new life in Christ proved more daunting.

The first adjustments we face as fledgling believers concern those closest to us–spouse and family. I thank God that in my case, those first adjustments were cause for rejoicing! The Lord engineered a marriage-saving change in my wife and me, and our two children at the time, Larry and Janet soon gave their young hearts to the Lord, too.

The challenge of the workplace however, can be a different story.

I had been employed at General Electric for eight years at their west-Toronto factory when I became a Christian. I came up through the ranks and had a supervisory position on the afternoon shift. It was often an extremely stressful job. I handled it by hard work, relentless energy and occasionally, I think, by brute force. I was a very profane person, especially so when things went wrong, and they frequently did.

On my first shift as a Christian, everything did go wrong...at the same time! There were personnel problems, a key machine broke down and the all-important production line was at a standstill.

I tore into the repair and remedial strategies with the usual aggressiveness, cursing with a well-practiced thoroughness all the while.

In time, the problems were brought under control and the production line resumed its monotonous journey. I grabbed a coffee and headed for my office to catch up on the reports, when suddenly, I was overwhelmed by a mega-ton of guilt! I saw the picture far, far too clearly. When familiar job pressures mounted, I reverted to habitual responses, namely, anger, impatience and vile, unbridled profanity. Greatly distressed, I pleaded with the Lord for His forgiveness. I felt assured that He had forgiven me yet a heavy sadness persisted. The problem was, my behavior patterns were thoroughly ingrained over the years and I had absolutely no confidence they could change, especially the swearing. Finally, in desperation I prayed something like this, "Lord, if You can make me feel so badly after I've sinned, couldn't You, by the same power, warn me ahead of time, instead?"

The gracious Lord swiftly answered that request. Thereafter, whenever a situation arose, in which I could be tempted to lose control and swear; something came up before my face. Something like two hands signaling stop, a reminder from the Lord to stop, and trust Him. Praise God, the swearing habit was conquered before the week was over!

Coming to Jesus was such a wonder to me I began to tell some of my friends that first day. A few were genuinely interested; others nodded but didn't want to discuss it. A few of the guys apparently wanted to make it the company joke.

"Well, Slim's got religion, who'd have thought it?" they guffawed. "Hallelujah! Praise the Lord!" They'd yell when I came by.

I learned something; good marks for a bold witness, but don't cast your pearls before swine, either.

Eric, a foreman I knew well sought me out. "Lee, I've heard you're a Christian, now. Is this true?" he asked.

"Yes," I replied, "I've accepted Jesus Christ as my Savior."

"Praise God!" he exclaimed, "That's wonderful! I'm a believer, too."

I was truly surprised. "Eric," I said, "We've known each other for eight years; I had no idea you were a Christian. You certainly knew I wasn't one; how come you never told me about Christ?"

Eric's face turned beet-red. Without a word, he turned and stomped away angrily.

A couple of hours later he returned and apologized. "You made me feel so guilty and ashamed," he explained, "but you're right, I should witness more, and I certainly should have shared the gospel with you."

I learned that it's important to let others know of your faith; it's also important to be gracious when dealing with someone else's shortcomings.

One of the first people I met when I hired on at GE was a young man named Max Hayward. Max and I soon became good friends. We were surprised at how many interests we had in common, even though Max is a Newfoundlander and I hail from Saskatchewan. I was anxious to share the news of my conversion with my good friend.

Max seemed quite unimpressed at my report. "Well, that's good," he said, offhandedly.

"That's not good, Max," I exclaimed, "that's wonderful! The Lord has changed me! I'm a saved man, now!"

"Well, yes, I understand what you mean," he replied, "My dad and others in the family are Christian believers, too."

"But what about you, Max?" I asked earnestly.

"I just don't feel that it's my time to make such a commitment," he said, "Perhaps later I will." Max was polite but adamant. I was perplexed. He was such an intelligent and decent man, and he had a Christian heritage; how could he resist the mercy and grace of God in such a way?

Eventually I moved back to Saskatchewan and more than 20 years after my conversion I received a note from Max. "Just wanted to let you know," it read, "I've finally accepted the Lord Jesus. I don't know why it took so long, but I'm a saved man, today."

God has the will. God has the way. God also has the time. No doubt, the Holy Spirit had been calling Max from early childhood. Jesus is well able to draw people to Himself, even if it takes two decades.

Before long, I learned another valuable lesson. Sometimes, what we regard as a personal strength is in reality a dangerous weakness that can carry us into ungodly behavior, and stall our spiritual growth.

Manny, a former professional boxer from Brazil worked in our department one Friday night. He had received his lay-off notice that day, and was filled with resentment. He went to a local bar during the supper hour and had a few drinks.

Marco, one of the machine operators, came to me later in the evening. "Manny is mad at everybody and he's roughing-up some of the guys," he reported. Marco had a red welt on the left side of his face.

I felt hot anger stirring inside me. I called the disgruntled South American over and quickly confronted him.

"Mind your own business!" he growled.

"Listen Manny," I retorted, "I'm not asking you I'm telling you; leave the men alone!"

"You gonna make me, gringo?" he snarled. He put up his hands, and cuffed me across the face with a very fast left. The blow sent my safety glasses flying.

Old instincts surfaced swiftly. I stepped in close, feinted him out of position, ripped a short right to the ribs and brought the left hook over, hard.

Manny pitched forward; I caught him before he hit the concrete floor, and heaved him onto a low worktable nearby.

In a few minutes, he revived and sat up sputtering and cursing. "You don't have to kill a guy, for God's sake," he whined.

I was nose-to-nose with him now. "Don't ever lift a hand against any of these men again!" I said. "You got that?"

"Yeah, yeah, I got it," he muttered as he hustled away.

I felt good, real good! Justice was served, wasn't it?

Then, it happened again; I was stricken with a suffocating sense of guilt! Something or someone spoke from deep in the center of my chest. It wasn't audible but I heard it clearly… "What about the other cheek?"

I was reeling now; I tried lamely to justify my actions. "Can't a man defend himself?" I asked out loud. It was useless; I knew I was guilty. Jesus would never have done what I did. This was simply the 'old Slim' settling things the way he always did. There was no evidence of a new life in Christ here at all. I discovered there, that what had been a strength for me when I was an unbeliever, was now a gross liability, as a follower of Christ. "Please forgive me again, Lord," I pleaded, "Give me another chance."

The Lord forgave me quickly, He also gave me another chance, and it wasn't far down the road.

Coming to Christ in repentance and faith is the wonderful commencement of a new and eternal life in God. The entrance into this spiritual life is entirely supernatural. The progress and growth of the Christian life also depends on supernatural influence.

CHAPTER 3

JESUS AT GROUND LEVEL

A lot of folks wonder if Jesus cares whether we have a decent job or not, or if He will help us to succeed at our work. Does Jesus get involved in the ordinary affairs of daily life down at ground level, where we live?

I understand that sometimes Christians get laid off; sometimes they run out of money, sometimes they go bankrupt. These things are part of life on this planet, and we believers are not exempt from hardship, at times. I also have come to understand, through many years and much experience, that the Lord is intensely concerned about every aspect of human life. Although eternal issues are undoubtedly in a class by themselves, it is not just in spiritual matters that we can turn to the Lord. If we can trust Him with our eternity, surely He is to be trusted with all the challenges we encounter day by day.

Of course, He expects us to apply ourselves and to work hard, just as He expects us to use common sense. However, He is ever-present to provide guidance and capability if we will surrender to Him and believe in His working on our behalf. I have observed this to be true through years in public ministry. I have found it equally so in the workplace and in the business world.

On several occasions in my life, I was an advertising sales representative. I sold ads in both print and electronic media. One winter while I was working for a city newspaper, the national economy slipped into a serious downturn and our sales revenues virtually dried up. Businesses were scaling back and the advertising budget was the first to feel the axe. Our daily sales-staff meetings were grim.

One morning, after the meeting, the Sales Manager asked me to remain while the rest of the reps went out.

"Look at this graph," he said, gesturing to the wall-sized graph detailing every sales person's, last years, projected, and current sales figures. "Every person's sales have steadily declined for the past six months, except one...yours! Your sales have held steady, and actually increased. I'd like an explanation. Is there something you know that the rest of us do not? Is there something you're doing that we should be doing?"

I was thoughtful for a moment, and then I replied, "Yes, I believe there is something I am doing that perhaps the others are not. And I do have a strategy in place that I'm sure would benefit everyone."

"Great!" the manager exclaimed, "I knew it! Will you please tell me what it is?"

"Certainly," I responded, "This is what I do day by day; I pray a lot, and trust the Lord Jesus for his help."

"Oh," Jim said weakly, "I should have known...you're going to talk to me about Jesus, again, aren't you?"

"I've got to be honest about it, Jim," I answered, "I work hard and do the best I can, but a lot of the other guys do that, too. The difference is Jesus. He helps me and I can't take the credit for that."

"Well, I can't argue with it," said Jim, "the figures are there on the wall."

Chapter three, verses five and six of Proverbs, reads like this, *"Trust in the Lord with all your heart and do not lean on your own understanding. In all your ways acknowledge him, and he will direct your paths."* This truth applies in every area of daily life. The Spirit of God can supply a flash of insight in a critical situation. He can infuse us with courage and strength to carry on when we are confused and defeated. He can help us to find favor and acceptance with people we deal with. In addition, if we are willing and obedient, He will arrange plenty of opportunities to share the truth about the Savior wc serve.

I began a career as a freelance illustrator when we lived in the Toronto area. At first, I did artwork part-time, but gradually volume increased and I was able to maintain my own studio at home, full-time. I specialized in illustrating the aboriginal peoples of early Canada. It was a very busy but enjoyable time of my life.

I had secured a major commission to illustrate graphics for eleven programs on Educational Television. The programs were aired nationally and across the U.S.

The graphics caught the interest of a large national firm in Montreal. They contacted me wondering if I would be interested in producing a large number of full-color paintings for a project they had in the planning stage.

Would I be interested? Would I be interested? I would be overjoyed! I would be ecstatic if I could land a commission like that! However, this was business and these things must be handled carefully and close to the vest. I indicated that I would give it serious thought.

Several officials from the company made plans to come to Toronto and invited me to join them for dinner at the Park Plaza. We could talk more...

The dinner was excellent; the conversation was amiable. I submitted that I had been working with Dr. E.S. Rogers of the Royal Ontario Museum for several years and would like it very much if he could be included in the project as the ethnological authority.

They had hoped to engage an ethnologist from Montreal but agreed to reconsider and perhaps contact Dr. Rogers, themselves.

About a week later, I received another call from Montreal inviting me for lunch there, to pursue our discussions and for me to view their facility.

We had another fine meal at a posh Montreal restaurant. I was informed that they had talked with Dr. Rogers, and indeed, he would be involved. Our discussions were very cordial; everything was fitting into place, except for one unsettled element...the artist's fee. What would I charge for my work? And, what would they be prepared to pay?

This issue had to be resolved, and it seemed to loom larger than it should have. I could see that they definitely wanted me to illustrate for them. On my part, I certainly wanted the job, but because of inexperience, I had no idea what to charge them. The company officials said they did not hold to a standard fee and were not prepared to mention a figure. We decided to meet in two weeks to negotiate a financial agreement.

In those two weeks, I tried to discover what other artists would charge for similar work. I got a lot of different answers. Although I had only been a Christian for about a year, and was not spiritually mature, I decided to seriously pray and put the matter in the Lord's hands. It was a sensitive issue. If my price was too high, I wouldn't get the job. If it was too low, I could stand to loose my shirt.

In two weeks, again I flew to Montreal. This time we met upstairs in the director's office. The place was huge and lavishly appointed. There were five men from the company, present. Most of them I had met before. All were university graduates. One man, Charles, had a Ph.D. The director, Franz, had two doctorates. I was a kid from the bush in northern Saskatchewan, facing off with this corps of heavy-weights. I was not alone, however, for the Lord was making His presence real to me. Though I didn't really know what I was doing, I was at peace and actually felt quite confident.

I had, at their request, brought a number of samples of my color work. The pieces were spread out on the polished mahogany desk. The men all examined them and voiced approval. Charles scrutinized several pieces very closely. "This is very fine work!" he said, "Excellent! The quality is fully equal to that of Henri Martin."

"We paid Henri, one fifty," one of the men I hadn't met before remarked, "That's the most we've ever paid."

There it was! Intentionally or inadvertently, I don't know, but finally a figure was out in the open! It wasn't totally unreasonable, but I felt I would require more.

The group watched me like vultures, waiting for a response.

I actually didn't know what to say then, so I casually took a seat in the director's plush chair and began to carefully put the artwork back into my briefcase piece by piece.

That act changed the dynamics of the whole room, instantly! They understood packing the artwork into the case to be a signal that I rejected the deal, outright.

The five, to a man, appeared very unsure of themselves, even distressed. All were on their feet, several paced.

I sat back in Franz's chair; I sensed the Lord very near and I was much at ease.

"Gentlemen," I said, finally, "your requirement is for extremely detailed illustrations, in fact an artist would have to work mostly from archival resource material, which would be time consuming. Furthermore, the time outlay for research in order to insure the necessary ethnological accuracy boggles the mind. Can you see that a fee similar to what was mentioned could not compensate for the time expenditure?"

Heads nodded. "You're right of course," Franz replied, "I can see that. Can you suggest a figure you would consider appropriate?"

"Perhaps twice that amount," I suggested.

There was a pause, and a few exchanged glances; Franz cleared his throat. "We're prepared to accept that figure," he said.

"I think we should discuss the matter of expenses, too," I remarked.

"By all means!" the doctor responded, "We'll supply an open-ended expense account."

"These are very reasonable terms, which I would be happy to accept," I declared.

"They are fair and reasonable terms," Franz observed, "let's call it a deal!"

I think a collective sigh escaped every one of us. There were smiles and handshakes all around. We signed a couple of documents, and soon I was six miles up and speeding west toward Toronto at 400 plus miles per hour.

I leaned back in the seat. Looking out the planes window the stars looked somehow closer that night. I rejoiced! I praised God! "Jesus," I prayed, "what a Negotiator You are! This is all Your doing. How I thank You!"

It was amazing! I left that meeting with a contract that was twice a large as any ever issued in the history of that national company. Furthermore, I was being paid twice the rate their highest-paid artist had ever received!

I don't think I ever enjoyed a flight as much as that one. I smiled a lot, at no one in particular. I have a hunch the Lord Jesus was smiling, too.

CHAPTER 4

TAKING A NEW DIRECTION

Most Christians pray for guidance and direction from time to time. The answer to such prayers may come in a strange way, sometimes in a very strange way. The spiritual direction of our family took an entirely new direction one evening, because of a little ball of wadded-up paper.

Our family attended First Baptist Church in Aurora, Ontario for about our first three years as Christians. Through the family music ministry, we met some Pentecostal people who told us about an experience called, the baptism in the Holy Spirit. They also informed us that Jesus still healed the sick and performed miracles today in response to prayer. Our church did not teach about these things, but we were very interested, mainly because the folks who spoke to us, obviously possessed a power and a reality in life and ministry that was largely absent in ours.

One Sunday morning as I walked through the base-ment auditorium at church, I noticed a small, balled-up wad of paper on the floor. I scooped it up and shoved it into the pocket of my suit jacket. (Just as any good Baptist deacon would do). That evening, at home, I rediscovered the tightly wadded ball of paper. Out of idle curiosity, I carefully unrolled it and discovered it was an invitation to a gospel meeting in Toronto that week with evangelist, T.L.Osborn. It was touted as a meeting where sinners would be saved, the sick would be healed and the miracle power of Christ would be demonstrated. Something went through me as I read those words. Something like a flash of excitement.

My wife, Bev and I read and re-read that invitation. We talked about it repeatedly. We alternated between being excited about, and disbelieving its claims entirely. After all, our church taught that healing and miracles ceased with the death of the Apostles.

Our two oldest children, Larry and Janet, soon took part in the discussion.

"I don't think we should take the children into a questionable meeting," my wife cautioned.

"We're not scared of that," Larry interjected. "What if it's all true? What if it's real?"

"Yeah," I muttered, "What if it is real?" Many questions percolated in my mind. This is the very thing we've been wondering about. This could be a way to find out the truth about these claims of healing and miracles. Maybe God is leading us in this, how can we afford to miss it? How could literature like this find its way into a conservative Baptist church? Moreover, how is it that I'm the one who picked it up?

Our whole family wavered over whether or not to attend that meeting, until the very day arrived. Just before supper I announced, "Well, we're going to decide right now about this gospel meeting. I say we go. How do you all feel about it?" Perhaps surprisingly, all were in favor, Larry the most emphatically so.

We made our way into the heart of the city and located the auditorium. A building that seated several thousand. The place was over half full when we arrived, and there was a definite sense of excitement and expectancy that I had not experienced before at a religious meeting.

Soon the orchestra began to play and a song leader led in some spirited faith-choruses. No funeral dirges here! I thought. I glanced around; the building was now packed and some folks were standing at the back.

After a while Daisy Osborn, the evangelist's wife came on-stage and took leadership of the service. She

18

encouraged us to stand and praise the Lord with our whole heart. The response was thunderous! It was totally foreign to me, yet it seemed so right, so completely appropriate. I actually wanted to raise both hands and shout, myself, but could not. My own religious bondage kept me silent.

I stole a sidelong glance at the children; they seemed to be enjoying it outright. We couldn't escape anyway, the chairs were close and we were in the middle of a row. Here we were...a little Baptist family trapped in a raucous and rousing Pentecostal meeting, our first such experience.

Seeing that the rest of the family seemed to be taking it in stride, I decided to relax, trust God and go with the flow. After all, we were here scouting for truth. I would evaluate carefully and determine whether this Pentecostal thing was real or not.

After a worship time of perhaps 45 minutes, Evangelist T.L.Osborn came to the microphone. He appeared to be a man of average height with slick black hair and piercing eyes. His voice was slightly high-pitched, but there was an electrifying quality about it. What I remember most vividly about hearing the man speak was the absolute certainty in the things he said, and the way he said them. This servant of God was speaking truth and he was utterly certain of it himself. He said, "Jesus Christ is alive from the dead and He's here! He's here to save! He's here to heal! He's here to set free every person in this room who will receive it!"

The crowd roared in agreement. A shiver went through me and the hairs on the back of my neck stood up...

T.L.Osborn preached for about three quarters of an hour. I had never heard such preaching in my life! The sermon content was Scriptural, positive, gripping, and mighty! He spoke with such boldness! Even more arresting than the ministry of the Word, was the wonderfully overwhelming power of the presence of Jesus among us that night!

At the conclusion of his message, the evangelist issued a brief appeal to those who would receive Jesus as Savior. The response was immediate and stunning. Several hundred streamed to the broad altar area around the platform. Some actually ran, many were weeping. The conviction of sin was powerful and penetrating.

At one point I looked up the aisle and saw a young woman in tears, start toward the front. She looked back and saw another young girl who had been with her, still standing at the back. She ran back, grabbed the younger girl by the hand and both ran to the front, weeping.

Osborn led the respondents in a mass prayer of repentance and faith. Workers mingled among the crowd, and new convert's literature was distributed. Soon the evangelist asked everyone to return to their seats.

He spoke again for about twenty minutes about why Jesus would now heal all who needed it, and were prepared to receive from His hand. He gave another brief appeal; again, surging humanity filled the space around the platform. I noticed some in wheel chairs, some on crutches.

T.L. explained that he would not lay hands on each person. "The Lord has shown me," he said, "that I am to pray a mass prayer, then we all believe God together and He will release His healing power among us to touch every one who will receive."

He proceeded to do just that. He prayed a brief but mighty prayer for healing and said, "Amen." Then Osborn said, "The Spirit of Christ is among us to heal and to set free! This is your time! Do what you couldn't do before! If you couldn't walk; in Jesus' name, rise up and walk! If you couldn't see before; open up your eyes in Jesus' name and look, and see!"

It was so simple, but it just happened, everywhere! I saw people get out of wheel chairs. I saw people throw down their crutches and leap and dance! People all around the altar area were laughing, and crying, and shouting, and praising God! It was a wonderful, and holy kind of bedlam!

That evening the Updike family came into a new understanding of the love of God and the power of His Christ. I, personally, have never been quite the same since.

We at last made our way to the car, through that excited, bustling crowd. We got in, closed the doors and, all talked at once! We had come to find out the truth, we all agreed we'd found it. We knew the Baptist way was good, but this was so strong, so right, so real, we knew we must pursue it.

On the way home Larry said, "I'm not just sure what the call of God is like, but perhaps I'm being called into evangelism. If I am," he continued, "I believe it's this kind of evangelism."

"Well, wouldn't you like to preach like Billy Graham?" I asked.

"No," he replied, "like this man."

CHAPTER 5

THE APOSTLE JIM

Jim Sleeth was five feet tall, but he was a big, big man. He had the upper body of a football lineman, barrel chest, thick neck, muscular shoulders and arms. However, life had dealt Jim a tough hand. At age three, he was stricken with polio. The aftermath of that once prevalent malady left him severely handicapped in the lower body. As a mature, man both legs were very underdeveloped, almost dwarf-like. He wore shoes fitted with springs that raised his toes at each step, because the muscles that should have performed that function were severely atrophied. For Jim, merely walking on level ground was slow and laborious; stairs were an almost impossible ordeal.

Though Jim truly possessed bodily weaknesses, those of us who knew him best soon forgot about physical things and recognized that this man was big for God.

Jim came to know the Lord when he was seventeen. As he told it, he was completely frustrated at trying to negotiate the teenage years as a cripple. He had heard the message of the gospel several times at the Stouffville Youth Center, and one night, in hopelessness, he lay on the floor beside his bed and cried to God, "Lord, help me!" Immediately, a strange peace came over him. He struggled into bed and slept. In the morning, the peace was still there. Later a friend, who was a Christian, helped him understand what had happened to him. He often said, the sinner's prayer he prayed only consisted of three words, "Lord help me," but it was enough for Jesus.

Jim graduated from the Canadian Bible College in Toronto. When I met him, he was a dispatcher at the Aurora Police Department. He attended the Associated Gospel Church, taught Sunday school at the Salvation Army and had founded a boy's club that met weekly to play various sports and have a Bible study. Jim was also available to sing and preach wherever he felt the Lord was leading.

It seemed Jim always showed up at crucial times, sometimes with a bag of groceries for a family in hard financial times. Once he just pulled into a farmyard as a husband stormed out of the house, in the act of leaving his wife. Jim persuaded the man to get into the van and talk for a while. After a couple of hours of talking, listening and finally praying, the two went into the house. Soon the Lord was able to restore the broken relationship. The man was later to become the Bible Class teacher of the little country church, nearby.

Periodically, Jim would take a vanload of food and clothing to a struggling native church on Manitoulin Island. Once in January, he was about to make the trip alone. Some of us thought it unwise for a handicapped man to travel alone so far north. I said, "Jim is this wise? The roads are poor and snow is heavy up there. What if you get off the road, or have mechanical trouble?"

"Well if any of those dire things happen I guess I'll just have to trust the Lord, won't I?" Jim replied, flashing his big grin. He swung up into the front seat of the van and headed north.

Through his police work, Jim had a lot of contact with hardened criminals, small-time crooks, and men who just took a wrong turn somewhere and ended up behind bars. Jim missed no chance to talk about Jesus to men in the cells, and steered many to a right course in life. I never had a special calling to minister to men in prison, but one day as I knelt to pray with five men in my living room, it occurred to me that every one was an ex-con. I came to know all of them through Jim.

From the beginning, Jim and I hit it off, and quickly became good friends. I suppose it was partly because we both had a desire to see people saved. Our idea of a good Saturday afternoon was to get out on the highway in his van, or my car and pick up hitchhikers. (The practice was not as dangerous in those days). A lead question Jim often asked a hitchhiker was, "Where ya heading?"

The person might answer, "North Bay," or "Kingston," or some other destination.

"I didn't mean, today," Jim would respond, "I mean, where are you heading when this life is over?"

The question was so forthright and direct that it often provoked a similar forthright response. It was quite amazing that within three minutes of having picked up a total stranger he would be talking freely about his eternal expectations. In those days, we witnessed about Jesus to many people, handed out a lot of gospel tracts and helped quite a few folks to faith in Christ.

Jim drove a Ford Econoline van; he considered it the Lord's vehicle. He had a typewritten statement taped to the dash on the passenger's side. It read something like this, "This is the Lord's van. You may sing, pray, praise the Lord, and enjoy good conversation here. You may not smoke, drink, swear, or engage in indecent conversation or behavior."

Periodically Jim held services on an Ojibwa Reserve on Georgina Island in Lake Simcoe. I accompanied him when I could. On one occasion, we took the ferry to the Island after lunch. "We'll canoe back if we miss the last ferry tonight," Jim explained.

We had a great afternoon and evening, conducting services in several homes. The people were very friendly and responsive. It was late evening when we finally got to the dock. The ferry had long gone and it was near dark. We started for the mainland in one of the canoes that were kept there for that purpose. We paddled for quite a while but did not seem to be getting near the shore as quickly as I thought we should. Soon we were in darkness and all we could see was a couple of lights on the distant shore. We must have drifted off course for soon we were entangled in a bed of dense reeds and nearly aground in shallow water. "Great spot," I observed, "aground in Lake Simcoe in total darkness in the middle of the night."

"Well," said Jim, "The same God who saved us and kept us this far, and who anointed us and blessed those people today, is still with us."

"Amen," I agreed, "and I guess it's time I got out of the boat." I took off my shoes and socks and began towing the craft. Jim, unable to walk in those circumstances, of course, used the two paddles like ski poles. Progress was slow at first, but we prayed and praised the Lord and kept making for the lights on shore. After about a quarter of a mile, we left the reeds behind and I was wading in deeper water. Soon the canoe floated freely. After another half hour of steady paddling, we hauled up on shore.

"This has been a day to remember," I remarked as we hit the road in Jim's van. "It was a remarkable time of ministry, then, a pretty stiff challenge. I have to admit I was a little uneasy out there for a while."

"We're in a war," Jim returned, "there's a real enemy. We gotta remember that when Jesus said, 'I will never leave you or forsake you,' He wasn't kidding."

A short time after I met Jim Sleeth, unknown to him, our family was in financial difficulty. The national client that I produced artwork for, as a freelance illustrator, had decided to withold payment for all commissions until the new fiscal year. I explained to the children, Larry and Janet, that we needed a miracle in our finances to get through the next few months. We prayed about it daily in our family devotions.

One Saturday morning, in the midst of our prayer time, there was a persistent knock at the door. I ignored it; after all, we were involved in serious matters. The knock continued. Finally, I went to the door, it was Jim. "I almost gave up," he said, "thought nobody was home."

"We're having family devotions," I explained.

"Well, can I join you?" Jim asked.

"Yeah, sure, you're welcome," I assured him, "come in and have a seat."

During Janet's prayer, she reminded the Lord that we were trusting in Him for a miracle, but did not elaborate. After the final amen, we sat and chatted a while.   Jim was thoughtful for a moment then he drew an envelope from his inside jacket pocket. "Is this is the miracle you have been praying about?" he asked, and handed the envelope to me.

I opened it and found five brand-new, one hundred dollar bills! (A lot of money in those days). "Jim, what's the meaning of this?" I asked incredulously.

"Tell me," he replied, "is this the miracle Janet prayed about? Is it a money problem you folks are facing?"

"Well, yes it is," I conceded.

"This is your answer," Jim said, "I hope it meets the need."

"Wait a minute!" I protested, "We hardly know each other. I can't take this kind of money from you like this."

Jim grinned. "Sure you can," he said, "It's how the Lord does things sometimes."

"How did you know about this?" I asked, "And more importantly, why would you do it?"

"Well, it's like this," he began, "I suspected for some time that things were tight for you. Yesterday I prayed and asked the Lord to help you financially. Something inside of me spoke and said, 'Why don't you help?' I argued that I did not have enough money myself to make much difference. Then I picked up my mail and found a letter from a finance company assuring me that my credit was good with them. Immediately the same voice said, 'Borrow five hundred and deliver it tomorrow.' So there it is," he said.

"You mean you borrowed five hundred dollars from a finance company for people you hardly know?" I exclaimed, "That's not very wise is it?"

Jim grinned again. "I think it's wisdom." he said, "God's, not mine. Do you folks think this is the answer to your prayers? Is it God's doing?"

The whole family was overwhelmed; we knew it was God! We could feel His love in it. Strangely, we had prayed for a miracle, when it happened we didn't know how to handle it. Truly, the Lord had answered our prayers in a miraculous way, and the need was fully met. Eventually my long overdue check arrived and I was able to repay Jim.

Jim confided later that, at the time he had no special feelings at all about his part in our miracle. To him it was simply a matter of naked obedience. Nevertheless, to us who received the benefit of his obedience–it was love. The truth of that experience has re-taught its lesson many times in my life. The realization that the Lord knew our need and could meet it in such a way, through someone we hardly knew– broke us up. We saw the love of God in it. We felt it.

Jim Sleeth had even more difficulty than I did in receiving the wonderful baptism in the Holy Spirit. He was an Evangelical through and through and didn't want much to do with the 'Pent-up-costals,' as he called the Pentecostal believers. I finally convinced him to rethink his position. I told him I had come to believe the baptism in the Holy Spirit was a valid experience for present-day believers, and I was earnestly seeking God for the blessing myself. Jim soon came onside and he, Bev and I spent many an evening in earnest prayer about it. At last I received the baptism, a few days later Bev, too received, about a week later Jim was wonderfully baptized and filled with the Holy Spirit.

His ministry was broadened greatly from that day, and took on an entirely new dimension. He was powerfully anointed and soon began to exercise spiritual gifts.

The Sunday after his personal Pentecost, he gave an appeal during his boy's Sunday school class at the Salvation Army. The whole class knelt that morning and received Christ as Savior. Several weeks later at the close of the final Boy's Club meeting of the summer, Jim presented a simple gospel message to the fifteen boys. Every one of them knelt there on the grass to receive Christ that evening.

Jim's preaching took on a new boldness and power. People often were deeply moved, and many were saved. He began to lay hands on the sick, and many were healed.

He and I ministered together many times. Usually I took the guitar and led the singing or accompanied Jim as he sang. He did most of the preaching in those early days. At one meeting, I led the singing; Jim remained in the back room to pray more. He seemed to take forever to make an appearance. I asked him about it later.

"It was the Holy Spirit," he explained, "I had decided to sing, 'I'd Rather Have Jesus,' but the Spirit spoke in my heart and said, 'If it isn't true in your life you shouldn't be singing about it.' I was staggered!" he said, "because right then I realized there were a few things in me that were not fully surrendered to Jesus. He had to do a new work in me before I could stand before the people in His name."

It often puzzled me how Jim could minister in the power of the Spirit and see people healed in answer to his prayers, yet he, himself was not healed. I wanted to talk to him about it but I never did until several years later.

Our family had relocated to Nipawin, Saskatchewan, and Jim had resigned his police job in favor of full-time, itinerant ministry. He traveled across the country and one summer, stopped for a few days at Nipawin.

In an evening, Jim and I were sitting out on the front step of our new home on Center Street. Danny, my youngest son was having a great time jumping off the step onto the grass. Jim became quiet and reflective. "How old is Danny?" he asked.

"He's three," I replied.

"I was three the last time I ran and jumped," he said quietly, "I remember that day. It was a beautiful summer day, just like today. I played outside, and I ran, I jumped, but in the evening, I felt sick. Mom put me to bed. I never jumped again, I never ran again, in fact I never had a normal life again."

"You've really been through some stuff, Jim," I responded, "and I'm totally in awe of what you're doing with your life and through your ministry."

"We all face stuff," he said, "it comes to different people, in different ways, at different times. But the Lord Jesus is with us every step of the way, if we trust Him."

"I've wanted to ask you something for a while," I said, "you pray for many people and they are healed, yet you have a serious physical need and the Lord hasn't healed you. How do you handle that?"

Jim looked sharply at me for a moment. "I've gone through some very deep water over that," he answered. "When we came into this Pentecostal way and saw the Lord healing and delivering people in answer to prayer; and later, when He began answering my own prayers for these things, I began to call upon Him for healing of my infirmity. I fasted, I prayed, I read the books and listened to tapes, I sought prayer from evangelists with healing ministries. Nothing happened! I became very preoccupied with myself. I visualized all the great work I would do for God...after He healed me. At last I was thoroughly discouraged," he explained, "I felt God was discriminating. Surely, He loved others more than He loved me. I told Him if He would not heal me, I could no longer minister for him. I reasoned that it was hypocrisy to attempt to minister to others what I was unable to receive, myself."

Now he spoke softly, with the ragged strain of anguish in his voice, tears came,

"With that foolish decision, I entered the darkest period of my entire Christian life. The peace was gone. The joy was gone. The reality was gone. It seemed like God, Himself was gone. I could not bear it, I thought of suicide. Finally I came to my senses and asked the Lord to forgive me for my selfishness," he went on, "I told Him I wanted His will, not mine. I said all I wanted was to please Him, to walk in His presence again, and to serve Him one hundred percent with whatever He gives me.

"I didn't hear Him speak but the love, the joy, the peace and the reality of His presence flooded back greater than I've ever known it. He's been blessing me, and leading me, and using me at a new level ever since, and how I praise Him for it!" he said. "Of course it would be great to be healed," he continued, "but if that's not to be for now, I'm content. Even if I never receive healing in this lifetime, I'll still rejoice and praise Him for who He is and everything He's done for me!"

Jim traveled across the country preaching, teaching, singing, conducting children's meetings, ministering on Indian Reserves.

Eventually he married, later had a son, John. The Sleeth family purchased a truck and trailer and continued to travel and minister for Jesus.

One fall Jim and his little family moved to England, where the ministry continued to be fruitful. On a rain-swept highway one night, the left front tire of the truck flipped up a broken piece of metal from the road; it lodged in the steering linkage and jammed it. At the next curve the vehicle rolled. Damage was minimal and everyone was okay, except that Jim had received a nasty bump on the head.

Later that night Jim suffered a massive stroke. Sadly, his once remarkable mind was almost completely incapacitated. He never recovered. Eventually he was placed in a care facility, and there he died.

To me, the passing of my friend, Jim Sleeth, seemed a tragic mistake that had been visited upon an extraordinary human being, the senseless termination of a fine and fruitful life. Only God knows the why of such things. We humans do not.

Though death came far too early to Jim, nevertheless, across the country he left the legacy of a host of people who had a genuine encounter with the Lord Jesus Christ. It was not just the preaching, we saw the reality of a life being lived for Jesus. The influence Jim Sleeth had on my early Christian life was profound. I miss him.

CHAPTER 6

THE GOOD SHEPHERD IS HERE

My dad, Ryburn Robert Updike, was born in a small community on the outskirts of Chicago on 6 November 1897. I recorded some of his history in the book, *Edge Of The Wilderness,* but the spiritual aspect of his life is much harder to nail down, mainly because he was disinclined to talk about it.

Apparently, Dad had a meaningful experience with the Lord when he was about fourteen. However, he lost sight of the God he knew, on the bloody killing fields of France, as he fought with the U.S. Army in the First World War. The teenaged soldier could not see a loving and compassionate God in the midst of unrelenting and unspeakable atrocities. I do not believe he rejected God outright but certainly, he withdrew his commitment and his trust to a place where it was threadbare, if it truly existed at all.

Some years after the war, Dad took up homesteading in the bush of northern Saskatchewan. Five or six years later, he met my mother, and they were married on June 1, 1929, at Saskatoon.

My parents were wonderful people; friendly, helpful, great neighbors and well thought of in the community. However, spiritual things were just never discussed in our home. We never went to church, and really didn't associate much with folks who did.

As long as I can remember, Dad was not well. He was plagued by serious stomach problems and was often hospitalized because of it. He surely possessed the wisdom, the experience, and the strength to transform our wilderness homestead into a productive farming operation, but his reoccurring health problems always laid him low. I know he was very discouraged at times, perhaps even embittered. In retrospect, I believe he spent most of his adult life in controversy with Jesus.

In time, my sister, Jean and I left home. She and her husband, Nick lived at Prince George, BC. I lived with my family near Toronto. This left my two younger brothers, Harley and Dale at home in Saskatchewan.

Jean and I both became Christians. Soon I took my family on a holiday trip home, but the main reason for the trip was to witness to my parents and my brothers about the Lord Jesus. Mom and Dad were both very cool to the gospel. In fact, dad was almost hostile.

One day I received an urgent phone call from Dale; Dad had suffered a heart attack and was in hospital at Nipawin. Of course, we prayed fervently, and enlisted the support of other praying people, as did Jean in Prince George.

While Dad lay in the emergency room of the Nipawin hospital being examined by medical staff, he suffered a second, massive heart attack and died. At least physically, he died. As he told me later in the many conversations we had about this experience, he simply vacated his body. The inner person, with all sense and intelligence, drifted upward to a place about ceiling height. He was not sure if he was above or below the ceiling, he found that in that state, matter just…didn't matter.

He observed the medical team working feverishly to resuscitate him, using all the techniques and technology of the day. Finally, all activity slowed; the heart monitor was static. A nurse announced, "There is no pulse." Another said, "There is no respiration."

Eventually all efforts ceased. There was somber talk, recording time of death, and other details discussed at such a time.

Dad said he thought of calling out, "Hey! I'm up here!" But, he realized they could not have heard him for he was in another dimension.

He told me that every aspect about where he found himself was immeasurably more wonderful and awesome than any concept he had ever entertained about such things! The focal point of everything was the light. He described it as being indescribably beautiful and intensely bright, yet not hurtful to the eyes. He said, "The light was Jesus." He didn't say that Jesus was at the center of the light, or that light emanated from Him. He said simply, "The Light was Jesus."

Dad was agonizingly aware that he was not connected to the Light, as though a great chasm separated him from it. At the same time, he had an overwhelming desire and a visceral longing to come to that Light.

I believe the precious Jesus, in the language and imagery of another world, was extending a hand of grace for forgiveness and recovery from the decades of misunderstanding, rebellion and bitterness.

Dad desperately wanted to cry out to the Lord for His help and forgiveness, but he was somehow fearful that there would be only one opportunity. In anguish and fear of failure, yet consumed with a desire to be right with Jesus, he set himself to shout with as much volume as he could muster. He shouted and was astonished and horrified that his loudest effort became the faint cry of a tiny lamb!

A kind voice from somewhere said, "That was a feeble bleat."

Another voice replied, "Yes, but the Good Shepherd is here."

Only eternity can explain what happened next. Dad said that he was drawn immediately and wonderfully into the Light. It was as though he had become 'one' with it, and was overwhelmed with the love, the joy, the peace and the presence and reality of Jesus. All it took was a feeble, lamb-like cry!

I had always known my dad to be a strong, controlled man, yet he wept freely every time he tried to relate this experience. I had many questions, but he would hold up a hand and say, "I can't talk about this part." He was not given liberty to share some of the wonders he had seen and heard.

After a while, he couldn't tell if it was minutes, hours or years, he was brought back to the place, about ceiling height in the emergency room. His lifeless form lay still on the examining table.

He was told he would now resume his earthly life. Involuntarily, he re-entered his body and began to re-animate it. He said that after the limitless freedom of the Spirit-world, taking on a flesh and blood body imposed severe restrictions. In a short time though, he again adapted to earthly conditions.

He lay on the table, fully alive, fully conscious and fully whole! The Lord had not only healed his spiritual condition, but he was completely well, physically.

He made a remark like, "If someone will fetch my clothes, I'd like to go home now."

Sheer bedlam followed! The dead man was not only alive, but he was well!

The doctors kept Dad in hospital for a couple of days, testing and re-testing. They had the before and after results, but technology could not reveal what had happened in between. Dad merely explained that Jesus had healed him. He did not describe his journey beyond the veil. He felt somehow unsure that he had leave to talk about it immediately.

Dad earnestly prayed, enquiring of the Lord whether something as holy as this experience should be shared with an unbelieving world.

That afternoon Pastor Harry Meeds from the Free Methodist Church stopped by. He left some Christian literature. As Dad browsed through it, he read that someone said, "That was a feeble bleat." Another replied, "Yes, but the Good Shepherd is here."

From that time, Dad began to tell about his experience. That testimony was hard to believe for many, but who could refute it? It was documented. The man was dead, now he was alive, healed by the power of God!

The greatest miracle of all was that, at last my father was spiritually alive! The rest of us in the family were all Christians now, and had prayed for Dad for years. Now he was more on-fire for God than any of us! The man we prayed for, and preached to, now exhorted us to get serious about spiritual matters, to pray more, to tell others about Christ, more.

He told me once on the phone, "Pray like your life depends on it...it does!"

I have an old Bible of his. On the last page he scrawled in pencil, "Lord, it's good to be washed in the bathtub of your word!"

He read the Bible continually, and made up for lost time in his prayer-life. He often spoke of "making contact" in prayer. Apparently, he found that it was possible to pray and yet not contact God. That troubled him. He believed we should persist until we "made contact," and that true contact with God was always life changing.

A few years after Dad's miracle, death-to-life experience, he was afflicted with rheumatoid arthritis. He was pain-filled and very restricted in his movements. Despite cortisone injections and other medication, he could hardly dress himself, or even lift a cup of tea.

He decided to really pray and trust the Lord only, for his help. One day he "made contact;" an astonishing miracle followed.

I asked him to explain how it happened.

"I had been praying and meditating on Isaiah 53, especially verse 5." he said, "The last phrase in that verse, says, *'By His stripes we are healed.'* The Holy Spirit caused me to see that that verse, including the last part of it, applies to me, and it applies to me, now! I understood that if Jesus carried my sicknesses and pains to the cross, I don't need to bear them. If He paid the price for my healing, I should not have to pay it. That truth became so real to me I just praised Him," he continued. "I was lying on my back in bed at the time, just thanking and praising the Lord, when a fire from God settled on the top of my head. It slowly passed through my entire body, much like a grass-fire moves across the prairie when there is not much wind. When the healing fire passed out through the soles of my feet, the arthritis was gone too! Not only that," he concluded, "but all my joints are as flexible and free as they were when I was 16 years old!"

Dad had an appointment with his doctor the next day, a man he had known for years. Dad strode into the office and said, "Say Doc, what do you think about this?" With that, he bent over and put his palms flat on the floor.

"Hey! What about the arthritis?" the doctor asked in surprise.

Dad just grinned.

"Are you going to tell me that Jesus has done this?" the man queried.

"I'm totally well," Dad replied, "Who else could do a thing like this?"

My father was 71 when he died of a heart attack, was raised to life again, and healed by the power of God. He lived seven more years, and he lived those years for theGod.

One afternoon, when he was 78, he was not feeling up to par so his doctor friend said, "Ryburn, I'm putting you in hospital for a couple of days, I want to do a few tests." Dad was cheerful and agreed, the doctor told me later.

The next evening, just after six, the doctor stopped to chat with Dad for a few minutes. "Well Ryburn, how are you feeling tonight?" he asked.

"I feel great!" Dad responded, "I've never been bet-ter! I'm going home tonight."

With that, Dad smiled, lay back on the pillow and…went home.

CHAPTER 7

DISCOVERING THE HOLY SPIRIT

NOTE:

This chapter and the one that follows have to do with a subject that unfortunately, has sometimes been a source of contention among God's people–the baptism in the Holy Spirit. I clearly recognize the different positions, having occupied both.

It is good to remember that the gracious Lord leads some of us on one path and some on another; nevertheless, by His grace we are well able to love one another, differences and all.

These two stories are a testimony of the Lord's dealings with me. If your spiritual journey thus far follows a different path, I understand and fully respect that.

Our family attended a concert one Sunday evening at First Baptist Church. The Leadly family ministered, Dad played guitar, Mom and the two children sang. The Updikes were inspired that night. We felt that that was something we could learn to do for the Lord. That evening marked the beginning of the Updike family's singing ministry.

We already knew Janet possessed a remarkable singing voice, right from kindergarten age. We soon discovered Larry was specially gifted, too. Bev taught him to sing parts, and in no time, he was able to sing lead, tenor and alto. In the early years, I rarely sang, concentrating rather on guitar accompaniment and being group spokesman.

All of us took this ministry seriously and prayed a lot about it. We were well received in local churches, and soon traveled farther afield, providing special music at church services, concerts and crusades. Occasionally we appeared on radio and television.

At times, we shared the platform with other singing groups. In some, I detected a spiritual power that went beyond mere talent. I asked several how it was that such a compelling force seemed to accompany their singing. I was told they had received the baptism in the Holy Spirit, which was an impartation of a new power to minister for Jesus. They encouraged me to seek the Lord in prayer for the same power.

I had never heard of such a thing but the notion was intriguing, indeed. We surely needed more of the power of God, however He chose to supply it.

I discussed the matter with the leadership at our church. Several of them scoffed openly at the idea as being, they said, "Pentecostal heresy." One of the deacons explained that our denominational belief was that healing, miracles, speaking in tongues and such phenomena all passed away with the apostles.

At the time, I had no interest and little knowledge of various denominational differences. I was just happy to be a Christian and wanted to help others find the Savior, too. Since my Baptist friends, who were far more spiritually mature than I, were so adamant that they knew the truth about the Holy Spirit, I was prepared to let the matter rest.

About that time, however, we attended the T.L. Osborn meeting in Toronto and witnessed the power of God demonstrated in an unmistakable and a mighty way. This caused us to view issues concerning the Holy Spirit in a definitely un-Baptist way. Our family began to suspect that the baptism in the Holy Spirit was a real experience, and that it was for today. We wondered if it was for us. My friend, Jim Sleeth was also seeking for more of God in his life and ministry.

I pored over the Scriptures, and read everything I could get my hands on regarding the Holy Spirit. We overcame our fears and attended occasional evening services in various Pentecostal churches, mostly in Toronto.

Jim, Bev and I often prayed in the evening at our place, seeking the Lord for more truth and more power. Sometimes our prayer meetings lasted into the wee hours.

One Sunday evening after church, we discovered the radio broadcast of Willowdale Pentecostal Church, on CFGM. Pastor Gerald Morgan hosted two wonderfully uplifting programs. The whole family listened every week.

One Sunday our curiosity got the better of us. We just had to find out what this Willowdale church was really like. We piled in the car and headed down Yonge Street into North Toronto. We located the church just east of Yonge on Empress Avenue.

The place was crowded, and the meeting was electrifying! The music was powerful! The preaching was powerful! The sense of the presence of God was powerful! A number of people were saved and some were healed in that service. We were stirred, mightily!

That week I made an appointment with Pastor Morgan, and Jim and I explained our search for the truth about the baptism in the Holy Spirit. Pastor Morgan took us through many Scriptures and answered our questions. He laid hands on us and prayed for us. Neither Jim nor I received the baptism that day, but now we were certain we were on the right track.

During the previous year, many changes had taken place in our Baptist church. Pastor Filyer had been replaced. Though our ties with the church seemed less secure, we remained faithful to our commitments. Bev was a leader in Pioneer Girls, and women's ministries. I served on the church board, the music committee, the ushering committee, and taught the high teen class.

I am sure the leadership took a dim view of our being absent from evening services several times a month, and that we were fraternizing with, "those Pentecostals."

In the meantime, Jim Sleeth and I had organized and conducted summer outreach services at Lake Wilcox Resort, a few miles down Yonge Street from Aurora.

Though Jim and the Updike family carried a lot of the ministry load, we also used the ministries of a number of music teams and preachers, some of them Pentecostals. Over the summer, some folks had accepted the Lord, and we attracted a following from among the local residents. We secured the facilities of an unused church for the fall season.

One day I realized I had been seeking for truth about the Spirit's baptism, and seeking for the personal experience for over a year. Something seemed to be hindering me from receiving the blessing I sought so earnestly. I decided to take a more direct approach. I prayed to this effect, "Lord, this is as far as I can go. I know I desperately need more of Your power in my life. I believe the baptism in the Holy Spirit is for today, and I believe it is for people like me. Today, I begin to fast and pray to receive that blessing until I either receive it, or You show me clearly that it is not for me. In either case," I concluded, "I will accept the outcome and continue to serve You the best I can. Amen"

I took my Bible, a notepad, and a booklet about receiving the Holy Spirit, by, Selwyn Hughes. I went into an upstairs bedroom, fasted and prayed.

The first day nothing noteworthy happened.

The second day also brought no heavenly visitation.

On the afternoon of the third day, I was very tired. I had prayed everything I knew to pray, every way I knew to pray it. I had praised the Lord until my voice was hoarse. I just decided to wait...

At two o-clock, I became aware that a very strong sense of the presence of the Lord permeated the room. Images began to take shape before the blank wall I was facing, a vision was forming. It gradually became clear; then I saw Jesus! He was standing, chest-deep in a beautiful stream. He smiled and nodded for me to join Him.

This was a very strange experience, for I was seated, motionless on a chair, yet I was participating in the vision!

I stepped into the water. It was little above my ankles, at the shore. I found quickly, this was no ordinary water; it was the water of Life! The Holy Spirit! A wonderful and exhilarating power gripped my ankles. It vibrated and surged through my feet and ankles like high-voltage electricity. Despite the sensation of great power, it was not painful, and there was an indescribable sense of rightness about it.

Jesus motioned me to come closer.

I walked toward Him slowly. The riverbed was smooth and secure underfoot. As I went deeper, the feeling of that Spirit-Water traveled up over my knees and thighs. I was being filled with the Spirit just as a teacup is filled, from the bottom up. Soon the depth was well above my waist. The wonderful fullness was not just on the outside surface of my body; it penetrated completely through, as though I were made of sponge.

I stopped about four feet from the Lord. He smiled broadly, as though He really enjoyed what was happening. "All the way," He said.

I obeyed quickly, and stood before Him. Face to face with Jesus, what joy! What a holy privilege!

He moved beside me, put a hand on my back, the other on my chest, plunged me deeply under the surface and brought me up again.

Baptized in the Spirit! Immersed in the Spirit! Filled with the Spirit! Saturated with the Spirit through skin, through tissue, through bone, through organs, filled with the Spirit of Life in Christ Jesus, through and through!

I have had many blessed experiences in God over the years, but nothing quite like this! I was full of love, and joy, and peace, and Jesus was never more real! My entire inner being was full of love for Jesus. I thanked Him, I praised Him, I shouted! It was not enough, not nearly enough. It seemed like my own language was a bottleneck, restricting the love and praise I tried to express.

Finally, I understood why people who are baptized in the Spirit speak in other tongues—they have to! Human language, at such a time, is inadequate to love, praise and worship the Father and His Christ.

"The Father is seeking true worshippers who will worship Him in Spirit and in truth," Jesus said.

I knew I would speak in tongues, but I had no idea how to go about it. Then a clear thought formed in my mind, 'just start.'

I did. I uttered a strange syllable or two of the many that seemed ready and waiting; and the dam broke! A torrent of words of love and adoration and praise and worship tumbled out. The flow was rich and endless.

What a glorious release! I felt that for the very first time I was adequately and acceptably loving and worshipping the Lord. Even though I could not translate the words, I could feel in the heart of my spirit, the substance of the message rising heavenward. I continued worshipping the Father and the Son in this manner until almost four o-clock.

Finally, I was silent and sat quietly before Him. I did not want to move, lest I disturb the aura of fulfillment and soft peace that enshrouded me there.

Later that afternoon I called Jim. "Jim," I said, "The Lord has baptized me in the Holy Spirit and I've been speaking in tongues for nearly two hours."

"Fine, great," he replied. However, there wasn't much conviction in his voice. He confided later that he was actually disappointed that I had received the blessing before he did. "Well, since the Lord has chosen you to be His man of might and power," he said, "you can do the preaching at Lake Wilcox on Sunday, I'm not."

"Okay, I'll do it," I responded.

I asked the Lord immediately what I should preach. A brief, simple message came clearly to my mind, but I was so moved by it that I wept uncontrollably.

Later I asked again about the message for Sunday. Again, the outline of the same sermon flashed into my mind, again I wept. I turned to the Scriptures in earnest, hoping to find an idea for a sermon that I could preach with at least some composure.

On Sunday, I still had not found anything that seemed to make sense; in desperation, I conceded. I told Jesus I would preach what He had given me, and if all I could do was stand and bawl, and humiliate myself before the people, so be it.

There were about 40 present in the Lake Wilcox meeting that day. I felt at ease, but I had no idea what to expect.

As I opened the Bible, the Holy Spirit came upon me in a way I had never experienced before. It was not the overwhelming, engulfing power, as in the baptism experience. His presence was more intimate and controlled, but nonetheless powerful. I was instantly calm and confident; all uncertainty left. The Bible was never clearer, and I could sense the nearness of Jesus.

I preached that simple message, dry-eyed. I shed no tears but the congregation did. I issued an appeal for any who wanted to receive Christ as Savior. Without hesitation, eight people came forward…every one of them wept. No one had ever responded to an altar call of mine before.

I have been very different and my ministry has been very different since I received the Spirit's baptism I came into a new humility and dependence on the Lord, with a confidence that as I ministered, things would happen, and that He, not I, would make them happen.

In my personal experience, the baptism in the Holy Spirit, has been a new door opened to more of the reality of Jesus. It is as though the indwelling Spirit expresses Himself in a new and deeper dimension, especially in the area of revelation. To me, there came a fresh awareness of the reality of Jesus in the Scriptures, in times of prayer and praise, in facing temptation and hard times, and most remarkably, in times of preaching and praying for the special needs of others.

CHAPTER 8

THE SPIRIT FILLED FAMILY

In September 1967, our family began attending the Willowdale Pentecostal Church, just off Yonge Street on Empress Avenue in north Toronto. Reverend Gerald Morgan was the pastor; his assistant was Miss Ella B. Parmenter. The Willowdale Church was a spiritual powerhouse in those days. Many people were saved, healed and blessed there each week. The message of the baptism of the Holy Spirit was also well taught and demonstrated.

At that time our son, Larry was twelve, our daughter, Janet was ten. Our family had been Christians for about three years. While we were by no means mature believers, we were nevertheless eager to serve God, and were seriously involved in a family singing ministry. Bev and I had received the baptism in the Holy Spirit, the children had not. They were earnestly seeking the Lord for the experience, though they did not fully understand it.

On Easter Sunday morning that year, Janet announced, with a calm certainty, that the Lord had spoken to her and that she would receive the baptism in the Holy Spirit that day.

"Are you quite sure about this, Janet?" I queried.

"Oh yes," she replied quickly, "It's what the Lord said."

Janet was at ease and certain, but I was concealing some apprehensions. After all, I had made diligent search for six months to establish in my own mind that the Spirit

baptism was a valid experience for today's Christian. Then, I had spent another six months of even more diligent seeking before I finally received the baptism. Is the Lord going to speak personally to a ten-year-old kid and grant her the experience the same day?

Well, why not? I thought. If the Lord is going to do something special for a kid, why not Janet? She is a great person, she loves Jesus, she is very serious about spiritual things and she gives herself wholeheartedly in her singing ministry. On the other hand, I reasoned, if she has misunderstood and nothing happens, will her faith be damaged? At last, I decided that this was a matter to be left in the Lord's hands.

Janet was cheerful and expectant as we made the twenty plus mile trip from our home in Aurora to Willowdale. I, on the other hand, was kind of preoccupied and praying fervently in my heart.

The service that morning seemed even more powerful than usual. The worship time seemed to carry us to the very gates of heaven, and Pastor Morgan was mightily anointed as he brought the message.

About halfway through the service Janet began to cry and seemed to be in extreme distress. We changed seats so that she could sit between her mother and me. "What's wrong Janet?" I asked.

"I'm scared, I feel sick and there's something wrong with my eyes. I can't see!" she cried.

Something rose up fiercely in the heart of my spirit. I suspected a devilish assault of some sort against our precious daughter. I rebuked the adversary in Jesus' name and Bev and I laid hands on Janet and prayed.

In a few minutes Janet exclaimed, "Whew! That's gone! I'm okay now, I'm fine, I can see again."

I am not sure exactly what that episode was, but the devil is real and he has many ugly strategies. In any case, Janet was undaunted. "I hope Pastor Morgan doesn't preach too long today," she said, eyes sparkling, "I'm anxious to go to the front and receive the Holy Spirit."

"You're going to the front?" I asked.

"Sure," she replied, "As soon as the preaching is over I'm going up there and ask Miss Parmenter to pray for me."

"Wonderful!" I said (but I redoubled the prayer activity going on in my heart).

At the conclusion of his message, Pastor Morgan gave an invitation to any who might need special prayer. Janet was out of her seat in a moment and was the first person to approach the platform. She seemed very little as she strode down that aisle and quickly mounted the three platform steps. Her long, dark hair swayed with each purposeful step. She went straight to Miss Parmenter. The gentle old saint leaned forward and listened intently to the youngster's request. We could see her smile broadly, and then offer a few words of instruction. Together they raised their hands and began to praise the Lord, an elderly spiritual leader who had walked close to Jesus for a lifetime, and an openhearted child who desired to know Him better. Miss Parmenter laid her hand on Janet's head and prayed. In a couple of minutes, the small hands began to shake strangely. The body trembled. Two prayerful parents rushed to the platform in time to hear a small voice begin to praise and worship God in a language that only He could understand.

In the New Testament accounts, Jesus always blessed the children. He's the same Jesus...He still does!

It was a wonderful experience for Janet and a great day for us all. To be sure, we had a joyful ride home after church that day.

One might wonder what difference does the baptism in the Holy Spirit make in the life of a ten-year- old.

We soon noticed a number of changes the Lord made in our daughter. We observed the most striking and measurable one before the day was over. It had to do with the Spirit's anointing to sing. Larry and Janet had been singing together in public ministry for several years. Their voices blended perfectly and were well balanced. Bev taught them to sing parts; I played the guitar accompaniment. That Sunday afternoon I said, "Let's go through a few songs." I stroked a chord and we began. The change was startling! Janet's voice had taken on a seemingly effortless new depth and power. Larry was overwhelmed. He stopped singing. "Janet!" he cried out, aghast, "what are you doing?"

"I dunno," she responded, "just singing...I guess."

"No you're not!" he shot back, "You're singing a whole lot louder or stronger or something."

"Well I'm not trying to, Larry," his sister returned. "It's just that it's a lot easier to sing today. It just comes out kinda...better."

"Is it the Holy Spirit, Janet?" I questioned.

She nodded and said quietly, "Yes, it's the Holy Spirit. I'm different, and I really feel different when I sing."

Indeed, she was different, and when she sang about Jesus, she was wonderfully different! Powerfully different! In time to come, she was to influence many people for Christ by that special anointing of the Holy Spirit on a beautiful and yielded voice.

Larry, at this point, was torn two ways. First, he rejoiced in the blessing of God on his sister, but he also felt keenly disappointed that Janet, two years his junior had received the Holy Spirit first. Larry had sought the Lord earnestly, far more than Janet had, he had often received prayer ministry. Larry was never one to be negative or depressed. Even as a twelve year old, he tried to maintain a positive, faith attitude. However, the weeks and months wore on and still the blessing eluded him.

In July, we attended Lakeside Pentecostal Camp at Cobourg Ontario. Reverend Tom Gannon, a leader of the Assemblies of God, was the main speaker.

That old tabernacle could accommodate 2,000, and was packed to the rafters that first night. The worship time was rousing, to say the least. The speaker preached a mighty sermon on the necessity of the baptism in the Holy Spirit, and the need of power to walk in the Spirit, in these times. He concluded with an impassioned appeal to those who recognized their need of the Spirit's fullness. Larry quickly responded, went forward and stood before the pulpit in the center of that huge altar area. To my utter amazement, not one other person joined him there.

"I can't believe this!" thundered the evangelist as he peered over the pulpit to see only one young boy standing before him. "Is there only one small boy in this place who needs more of God? Is it just this lad whose heart is open to the Spirit of God tonight?" Still no one else budged.

"God bless you my boy!" he roared, "You have come for the blessing of God, and the blessing of God you shall receive!"

"Is there any man of God out there who will touch God for this young man?" the evangelist asked.

Finally, people came alive. About twenty-five or thirty pastors and evangelists crowded around my son to minister in prayer. They had him sit on the altar, which was about two feet high, then gathered around him about four-deep and began to pray. I felt confident that with all that prayer-power Larry would certainly receive the baptism in the Holy Spirit quickly.

Soon hundreds of others flocked to the altar to seek the Lord, but the center of it all was that group of men crying out for the blessing of God to come upon an earnest young lad.

I hung around that knot of praying humanity, trying to catch a glimpse of Larry through the crowd. At last, several people moved and I saw him...nothing was happening! He looked very discouraged, as though he wished he were somewhere else.

"Oh Lord!" I groaned, "Don't let him be disappointed this time!" My heart was heavy, I cried out desperately to the Lord. Then a voice seemed to speak in the center of my being. It was not an audible voice, nevertheless it spoke and I perceived it. The voice said, "Get Janet to pray for Larry." Absurd! Absurd! I thought. This can't be God.

I prayed more fervently. The voice came again, "Get Janet to pray for Larry." This was too clear to reject out of hand, "Lord," I prayed, "If this is You, please speak again."

"Get Janet to pray for Larry," the voice intoned.

"Thank You, Lord," I responded. This seemed to make no sense at all. Here was a host of some of the most spiritual men in eastern Canada praying for my son. What is his ten-year-old sister going to be able to accomplish that these men of God cannot? Besides, there were 2,000 people in the building and I had no idea where Janet was.

"Lord," I prayed again, "please show me where Janet is." There was no voice this time, but a "sense" a "something" that urged me to go to the left end of the altar. There, immediately, I found her kneeling and softly weeping before the Lord. I knelt beside her and said, "Janet, they're praying for Larry but nothing is happening. The Lord told me to get you to pray for your brother."

Janet didn't say a word, just rose to her feet. I led the way and she followed.

The next problem was there was such a crowd surrounding Larry, how could Janet get near enough to pray for him? "Oh Lord," I groaned, "Help us to get near."

As we approached that great shouting crowd, a man who had been seated next to Larry pushed his way through the crowd and left the group. A clear aisle opened up immediately. Janet never stopped, she just continued walking through the opening and sat down beside her brother. Here is another miracle...The Lord kept that opening clear so that I could see everything that was happening with my children. I watched Janet, a small, cute ten-year-old sitting on the altar. Her feet didn't touch the floor. She looked at her brother for a moment. He sat, eyes closed, prayerful. She reached up and tapped him on the shoulder. Larry opened his eyes, surprised at seeing his sister. I could not hear the words, but I read his lips as he said, "Janet, what are you doing here?"

She motioned him to draw closer. He leaned over and she spoke in his ear. He straightened up and looked into her face for a few seconds, obviously making a decision. Then as he raised his hands, Janet put a hand on his shoulder and prayed. To my extreme amazement, in less than 60 seconds Larry was baptized in the Holy Spirit and speaking in other tongues at the top of his voice!

The evangelist strode to the microphone, "Ladies and gentlemen," he bellowed, "the young boy has received the Holy Ghost!" A mighty roar of praise thundered through the old building as 2,000 voices united to thank and praise our gracious Lord for fulfilling the desire of one young heart.

Larry was very demonstrative of his joy in receiving the blessing of God. He leaped, he shouted, he danced! A number of youth were seeking the Lord at the right side of the altar. Larry laid hands on them and prayed, many were filled.

This was a marvelous and a miraculous evening! I was filled with rejoicing, but I also had a problem and Janet had the answer. I finally located her in the throng. I knelt in front of her. "Janet," I said, "what did you say to him?"

"Oh" she replied, as though it was something everybody should know, "I just said, 'say what I say.'"

So this is the wisdom of God, I thought, Larry thinks the Spirit is going to move his tongue and do the speaking. He does not realize the Spirit only supplies the words, and he has to speak them. As soon as he surrenders his known language and begins to follow the Spirit, he is filled and a new language flows.

The next day Larry and Janet sang together. Once more, there was perfect balance; both were anointed equally and powerfully. Because of the presence and the power of the Holy Spirit, their singing blessed and changed many lives throughout the years of their Christian ministry.

CHAPTER 9

DOUBLE BLESSING AT CHRISTMAS

In December of 1967, our little family appeared to be facing our bleakest Christmas, ever. With thousands of dollars held in abeyance by the national company that I had been commissioned to do illustrations for, our financial situation was extremely strained. Early that month I hired on temporarily at a small factory a few blocks from home, in order to initiate some immediate cash flow, hopeful that the remuneration for my artwork would be released early in the New Year.

It was time to be purchasing a Christmas tree; I held off, not wanting to spend precious dollars. After a generous snowfall one afternoon, I saw our small spruce tree in the back yard in a new light. It was a beautiful little tree, about three and a half feet tall. Larry and Janet had named the tree, "Bruce," Bruce the spruce.

That evening at supper, I raised the possibility of having Bruce as our Christmas tree that year. There was lively discussion. Janet thought it would be wrong to take Bruce's life for our own purposes. Larry thought it would be a worthy sacrifice, reasoning that it would be an honor for Bruce to lay down his life in celebration of the Lord's birth. At length the four of us came to a consensus.

We almost made a ritual of cutting down the tree. I cleared the snow away thoroughly and, using a handsaw, cut off the small trunk at ground level.

We installed Bruce the spruce on the coffee table and had quite a few decorations left over. Despite his small stature, Bruce was, every inch a beautiful Christmas tree.

Perhaps it's not so strange, but I'm sure that none of the family remembers specific trees from any yard we have ever had...except for Bruce. To this day, every one of us remembers Bruce the spruce. Maybe it's because of his sacrifice...

At the end of a Sunday morning service at the Willowdale church two weeks before Christmas, Norm, a man that I didn't know well, approached me. He seemed a little hesitant, perhaps embarrassed. "Brother Lee," he said, "we've ended up with two Christmas turkeys this year. Would you be offended if I offered one of them to you?"

"Heck no!" I assured him, "I'd be grateful. As a matter of fact we weren't going to be able to have a turkey at all this year."

"Well," he said, obviously relieved, "this really must be the Lord's doing, then. Something seemed to be telling me to give you this turkey; but I wasn't sure whether it was the Lord or my own thoughts."

"I'm sure thanking the Lord for it, Norm," I replied, "but I want you to know I really appreciate what you've done, too."

It was a nice bird, about eight or nine pounds, just right for a family of four. We rejoiced and praised the Lord that day for supplying a Christmas turkey we never expected.

Several days before Christmas the Superintendent of our little factory called the employees together at the end of the day. He gave a little speech in which he said, "It's been a good year. Not quite good enough to issue bonus cheques, but we do have a gift for each of you. Pick it up on your way out the front door. Wonder of wonders, it was another turkey! A premium-grade, twenty-five pounder, individually packaged in a cardboard box, with handles! I had never seen a turkey of that size or of that quality before.

Once again, the family rejoiced and thanked God. At first, we automatically assumed the bird was for us, but as the evening wore on, we all realized we could not keep it. Finally, my wife said, "We can't keep this turkey, can we?"

"No," I responded, "The Lord has already given us our turkey. This one is for somebody else. I'm thinking of the Marshalls. They have six kids and they don't have much for Christmas, either."

We all agreed to give the big turkey to the Marshall family, and we prayed about it together. Then we jumped in the car and went right over to the Marshall's place. "Folks," I announced, "this is a gift from the Lord Jesus. Merry Christmas and God bless you!"

The whole Marshall family crowded around. "Wow!" big Louie Marshall exclaimed! "I never seen a turkey that big in my life, its top grade too! But hey, we can't accept this, it's too much."

"No Louie," I said, "This is the Lord's doing. He's already given us a turkey; this one's for your family."

"Nobody's ever given us anything like this," Louie's wife said. "We appreciate it so much... We couldn't afford a turkey this year."

"We know how that feels," I replied.

The most wonderful part of what the Lord did among us in those days was that, later that year, the whole Marshall family gave their hearts to the Lord Jesus.

CHAPTER 10

A MIRACLE BEFORE BREAKFAST

From the earliest days of my Christian life, I have been burdened in my soul for people who have never met Jesus, and have tried often to reach out to them with the gospel. Through my soul-winning efforts in the town of Aurora, where we lived, I met the Marshalls, an Ojibwa family who had many problems. I talked about Jesus to Louie and Linda and encouraged them to let Him be Lord of their lives. They were very polite but quite cool to the gospel message. I prayed a lot for them and their six children, that the Lord would find a way to open their hearts. One day, at seven o'clock in the morning, there was a very unexpected answer to that prayer.

Our family was just finishing breakfast when the phone rang. I answered. It was Linda, she sounded hysterical. The commotion I could hear in the background was very disturbing. "Lee!" she screamed, "Come and help us. Louie's gone crazy. He's going to kill us all!"

"I'll be right there!" I yelled into the phone. I slipped a small New Testament into a shirt pocket, grabbed my jacket and sprinted out to the car. In moments, I was speeding across town toward a place where, frankly, I did not want to go.

I skidded to a stop and made my way quickly to the outdoor staircase that led to the front door of Louie's second-floor duplex. I took the stairs two at a time. The closer I got to the landing the more frightening the sounds of the ruckus going on inside became.

I hammered on the door. Nobody heard. I shoved the door open and stepped in. It was like a horror movie! Six children were crying and screaming in fear. The family dog was in a frenzy of growling and barking. Breakfast for eight was splattered about the room because the kitchen table and every chair had been overturned. Linda lay sobbing and cowering on the floor, and Louie stood over her bellowing obscenities. He had torn a leg off the table and was poised to cave his wife's skull in with it.

"What's going on in here?" I roared. My voice had a crackle and a sharpness to it that cut through the din like a bullwhip. I am sure it was the Holy Spirit Who had anointed me with such boldness. The moment I spoke, there was instant silence. The children scurried down the hall and disappeared into various doorways. The dog dropped its head and slunk away. Linda stopped crying. Louie stood motionless, like a mannequin, silently.

I strode quickly across the room and confronted Louie. "What do you think you're doing?" I asked, with the same biting voice of authority that I hardly recognized as my own.

The big man looked down. "I dunno," he mumbled. "I ...dunno." He realized he still held the table leg, and tossed it away quickly, as though it had suddenly become hot to the touch.

I helped Linda to her feet, then grabbed two chairs and set them upright against a wall. "You sit there." I ordered the two. They quickly sat down. I positioned another chair and sat facing the couple. I read a few passages of Scripture and proceeded to preach the gospel. They listened...they cried. The sermon was brief and I minced no words. "Well," I said, snapping the Testament shut and pocketing it, "the choice is yours. You can have Jesus, or you can have this." I gestured to the room that looked like it had been ravaged by a small tornado.

"We have to have Jesus," they said, almost in unison.

"Look," Louie continued, "I know everything you've said is true, and I believe Jesus is our only hope, but I don't know how to go about this, and I don't know if I can live the life."

"What do we do?" Linda sniffed.

"You make the choice," I replied, "He supplies the power. You don't have the power to change the way you've been living, and you don't have the ability to live in a way that pleases God. Jesus is the miracle worker. Your part is to repent and believe."

The Ojibwa couple freely and fully confessed their sins, repented before God and received Jesus into their hearts as Savior and Lord. Soon the three of us raised our voices heavenward in tearful and joyful thanksgiving for the greatest of all miracles. The room that, a few minutes before had been filled with fear and violence, was now filled with the presence and the joy of the Lord.

The children began, timidly, to return to the kitchen. When they saw their parents forgiving and embracing each other, they crowded around and received tearful and reassuring hugs, too. Even the family dog wagged his tail furiously, as he busied himself with the remnants of breakfast so conveniently at hand.

Some time later, after many hugs all around, I left. As I sat behind the wheel, I praised God with my whole heart for everything He has given us in Jesus, and for the faithfulness and power of the Holy Spirit to open closed and hurting lives to His love, mercy and grace.

CHAPTER 11

SURPRISED BY HIS GOODNESS

Several weeks after Louie and Linda met with Jesus, I got a phone call from Louie. "A woman we know tried to commit suicide last week," big Louie said, "overdose of pills. She is getting out of the hospital at one, today, and she sure needs Jesus. Can we bring her over so you can talk to her?"

"You bet!" I assured him, "Come here right from the hospital."

About one-thirty Louie's old car pulled up and the two new converts introduced their troubled friend, Mary Hall.

Mary was a slender woman of medium height, thirty-something, but she looked much older. Bitter years had etched their history on her inner life as well as her countenance. Her wispy blonde hair looked hastily combed, with obviously no effort made to style it. This woman, however, had one arresting feature, a set of pale, blue eyes. Although they held much pain, her gaze was frank and direct.

Without question, Mary Hall was a severely wounded person in a very fragile condition. I prayed fervently within myself that the Holy Spirit would maintain full oversight of everything that happened in our home that afternoon.

Bev had the coffee pot on and we all sat around the dining room table. I sat at the west end; Mary sat across the corner from me. She chain-smoked. Though did not permit smoking in our house, we made no effort to prohibit something that seemed to provide at least some comfort to such a shattered soul.

I did not intend to attempt any sort of in-depth counseling. My sole objective was to introduce her to the Lord Jesus Christ.

I asked a few general questions, and then said, "Mary, nothing is impossible with God. Even when, wherever we look, everything seems hopeless, there is always Jesus. He can work a miracle in any situation. I was preparing for my own suicide four years ago," I continued, "but I met the Lord Jesus, He healed my life and transformed our home."

"Well," Mary replied, "I guess the reason I'm here is because of Louie and Linda. Their home used to be a warzone, just like mine. Louie was drunk half the time, and they were always screaming and cursing at each other. But in the last couple of weeks, it's been heaven over there. Nobody's yelling, there's love in the place, you can feel it."

"Jesus has done a great miracle for us," Louie said, "Even the children are accepting Him one-by-one."

"And Louie's been healed of diabetes, too," Linda added.

"I don't have a clue how any of these things can happen to a person," Mary observed.

I opened the Bible and explained the wonderful way of salvation. I told her of the death and resurrection of Jesus, and of the power of His blood to cleanse away sin. I explained that when we receive Christ as Savior and Lord, He transforms us into new creatures.

Mary was very thoughtful for several minutes. "I can't deny that what you've said is true," she said quietly, "but I confess that I have no confidence that He would do it for me."

"Mary," I replied, "There is no one in this world that Jesus loves more than He loves you. He not only has the power to meet every need of yours, right here this afternoon, but He has a great desire to do so!"

The blonde woman was silent and thoughtful again. She took a last drag on her cigarette and exhaled a plume of smoke high over the center of the table. "Well then," she said, looking at me with that same steady gaze, "I really want Him, and everything He can do for me." She stubbed out her cigarette and sat back purposefully.

I asked her to kneel at the couch, and then in Jesus' name, I rebuked the powers of darkness that troubled her life, the spirit of depression, and of hopelessness and of suicide. I instructed her briefly about repentance and faith.

Mary Hall's prayer was astonishingly forthright and profound, for one who had literally no previous experience in spiritual things. She finally said, "Amen," rose to her feet and began to laugh! It was genuine, hearty, sidesplitting laughter. Soon tears were rolling down her cheeks.

A twinge of uncertainty came over me. I was not sure whether a spiritual transaction had taken place or whether this woman was mocking holy things. Finally, I said bluntly, "What's so funny?"

"It's so easy!" she exclaimed, gasping for breath. "So much of my life has been heartache and pain and trouble, just to think that I could have had Jesus all those years ago. And it is so easy!"

"Are you sure you have Jesus in your heart?" I queried, still a bit skeptical.

"Of course I'm sure!" she responded emphatically. "I can feel Him, right here," she said, patting her upper chest. "And I have a soft peace and a wonderful joy that I've never experienced before, ever. All of this is Jesus. I know it is. I love Him and I know He loves me! Oh, thank You, Jesus!" she cried.

The three of us joined Mary in thanksgiving and praise to the Lord for His wonderful grace and kindness. I felt ashamed of my earlier doubts. The Lord had done a deep work and I had not perceived it.

A week later I received a phone call from Mary Hall, "Lee," she said, "my daughter, Kathy, is a very troubled fourteen-year-old. I am praying that she will open her heart to Jesus, as I have. Can I bring her over to your place? I think she needs to hear one of your little talks."

"By all means, bring her over," I replied.

Within the hour, we were sitting around the dining room table. The young girl sat where her mother had sat, and heard the same message of the love of God. Soon she knelt at the same couch and received the same Christ into her young heart.

As the years passed, our family moved to Saskatchewan and we lost touch with many of our friends in Ontario. However, when Jim Sleeth traveled west on a ministry trip we were able to get updated news from Ontario. One of the first people I inquired about was Mary Hall.

"Mary Hall," Jim said, "has become a sensitive and mature Christian woman. She leads a Bible study, now. And guess what? Mary is a soul winner, too!"

CHAPTER 12

THE PERFECT FIT

We make many requests of the Lord in our prayers. Sometimes, when no answer comes, we wonder where the problem lies, not realizing that we ourselves are the greatest hindrance. The Lord may be reaching our way to minister to some need, perhaps in response to fervent prayer, but He may have to postpone our help until He first deals with some of the carnalities of our own nature. He taught me this lesson one December in Aurora, Ontario.

In the spring of 1967, I resigned my position as a Machine Attendant at General Electric in Toronto, in order to devote full time to a budding career as a freelance illustrator. That December, I had hired on at a small manufacturing concern in Aurora. Money was tight as thousands of dollars owed me by a major national client were being witheld until the following fiscal year.

The boots I wore to the new workplace were badly worn; in fact, there were holes in the soles of both boots. Each evening I would cut and install several thicknesses of cardboard as insoles, to prepare the boots for the next days work. No one knew of this except my wife.

One evening Louie Marshall and I drove down Aurora's main street and parked beside the café. The headlights beamed directly into the alley between two buildings.

"Hey!" Louie exclaimed, "There's a pair of boots in the alley."

"Well, they probably belong to someone who lives or works nearby," I replied.

"I'm going to have a look," he said.

"Leave 'em there," I retorted, "we don't need someone else's boots."

"Won't hurt to have a look," the big guy said, as he shoved the door open and crossed the sidewalk.

I felt strangely uneasy, even a little angry at what was happening. Why pick up someone's cast-off boots in an alley? I thought. They probably belong to some drunken bum. Why should Louie even bother to look?

In a few minutes, Louie returned, smiling broadly. "Man!" he beamed, "what a find! These are police boots, and brand new. Can I ever put them to use!" He jumped into the car and proceeded to untie his own boots and try on the newfound pair. "Heck!" he snorted, "they're too darned small, must be nines."

"Hey!" he went on, "maybe they'll fit you. What size d'you wear?"

"Naw, they'd never fit me." I returned. I felt a strange resentment over all of this. "Put 'em back where you found 'em," I said.

"You can try 'em on when you get home," Big Louie said, tossing the boots into the back seat. "Maybe the Lord is giving you a new pair of boots."

"I don't look in alleys for gifts from the Lord," I responded sourly. However, there was a faint gnawing sense, deep down, that asked the question, "What if he's right?"

Later I dropped Louie off and went home. I took the boots into the basement and tossed them under the stairs. I made a point of not examining them so I had no idea of their size or quality. I simply put them out of my mind.

The nightly ritual of cutting cardboard insoles continued for about a week and a half, then a serious emergency arose; the sole of the left boot cracked across its entire width, and the front half was beginning to detach from the upper. "Oh Lord," I prayed, "Please help me to be able to afford a decent pair of boots. I know there are other needs but this is getting critical."

From somewhere in the deepest part of me, someone seemed to say, "I've given you a pair of boots. Why do you despise my gift?"

My heart beat faster. I thought of the boots under the basement stairs. I crawled under and retrieved them. I sat on the third step and for the first time, carefully examined the boots. They were beautiful, police issue no doubt. I ran a hand over the smooth kid leather. They were new, brand new. I could not help trembling as I pulled them on. They fit perfectly...could it be otherwise? I was so ashamed I couldn't look up. "Oh Lord," I cried, "Please forgive me for my pride, stubbornness and ignorance. You have done such a kind and gracious thing for me, and I couldn't even recognize it and I wouldn't receive it." I laced up the boots and walked around the basement thanking and praising the Lord.

Need I say, those boots met my need perfectly, and they were the most comfortable pair of work boots I have ever owned. Furthermore, I had the joy of experiencing the Lord's personal involvement in my life one more time. Perhaps even more importantly, I received a penetrating lesson on humility from the greatest of all teachers.

CHAPTER 13

THE DEATH OF A SAINT

The eight months I worked in the small factory in Aurora proved to be a period that brought some tough challenges to my faith. It also presented many opportunities to witness for the Lord, sometimes in unexpected ways.

On my first day on the job, the foreman introduced me to some of the men I would be working with. One of them was Johnny Brighton. As we walked on after meeting Johnny, the foreman explained, "John is a hell of a good man, but he's one of those religious types, y'know what I mean…"

"Hmm," I replied with a nod, not wanting to pursue that.

At coffee break, I sought out Mr. Brighton. "They say you are a religious man, John," I said, "What do they mean by that?"

"I'm a born again Christian," he replied, "I suppose that would be it."

"Praise the Lord!" I responded, "I'm a Christian, too." We were both encouraged. At least there were two of us in the workplace. We shared coffee break several times in the next two weeks. Then Johnny missed work for a week. "He has been having some health problems lately," the foreman said, "misses a few days now and then."

The weeks went on and there was talk that Johnny was doing better and would soon be back. It did not happen. One Monday, just before start-up, the foreman announced that Johnny had been diagnosed with cancer, and was having a rough time. We all signed a get-well card and the company sent a basket of fruit.

Several months passed, then one morning the factory general manager called us together. "Johnny Brighton is in the hospital at Newmarket" he announced, "They say he's not going to make it. I've made arrangements for a bunch of us to go up and see him for a few minutes this afternoon," he continued. "We'll shut down at three-thirty for the day. Let's go up there and see if we can cheer him up a little bit."

The mood in the factory was definitely somber that day. Though I barely knew Johnny Brighton, some of the men had worked with him for over 25 years. Everyone remembered what a decent, friendly man he was, honest and generous to a fault, a great man to have for a friend. He would be leaving behind, a wife, and two young boys. It just did not seem fair.

At three-thirty, nearly 25 of us piled into half a dozen cars for the five-mile trip to Newmarket.

They had wheeled Johnny into a larger room for the occasion. Despite this, the room was crowded.

I was astonished at how emaciated Johnny Brighton had become in those months. He was a skeleton of his former self. The skin, stretched tautly over his bony face was a light, coffee-brown. His eyes, sunken in cavernous sockets, were dull and lifeless. It seemed he was drained of all vitality.

The general manager was first to approach Johnny's bed. On behalf of himself and the company, he expressed concern, assuring John that he was sorely missed and that everyone was pulling for him.

John thanked him weakly, but it was as though a corpse was speaking from the bed.

The G.M. invited the rest of us to take our turn and speak briefly to our former workmate. It was so sad to see the pathetic efforts of, even his long-time friends, to express their hearts to the sick man. None of these men knew Jesus,

65

and it was never more apparent than there, in the presence of imminent death.

Finally, it was my turn, "Hi Johnny," I said, "It's Lee."

"Lee," he exclaimed, "I was hoping you'd come."

Something strange was happening. Johnny Brighton was coming alive! His eyes were brighter. He moved his arms. His voice was stronger. "Sit on the bed," he said.

I sat, and my heart was broken as I looked at him, fully realizing how near death he was. "John," I said, "I've never been where you are today, I don't know how I'd ever handle it. But I've been praying a lot that you would be healed…"

"No, brother," he interrupted, "I've done a lot of praying, too. It looks like it has to be this way. I know the Lord is with me, and with His help I can face the fear and the pain, but its Marie and the boys…" Johnny began to cry, deep sobs from the depth of his soul.

I did not know what to do so I put my hands under his shoulders and lifted him to a sitting position. We just sat there, held each other, and wept great tears over the sadness that was befalling his little family.

Something supernatural happened to me there, I am sure it happened to John, too…we utterly forgot about the other 25 men in the room. It was just two brothers and Jesus.

"John," I said, "you've trusted Him all these years, don't stop now. He has watched over your family every step of the way while you have been with them, He will watch over them even more when you are not. You can trust in Jesus with your whole heart, and with your whole eternity, and you can trust Him with your whole family, too."

"I know it! I know it!" he exclaimed feebly, "but I just needed to hear that word again. Will you pray for me?" he asked.

I laid him back on the pillow gently and prayed everything the Spirit empowered me to pray.

"Thank You, Jesus! Thank You, Jesus!" John cried. "And thank you my brother, for coming," he said, "The Lord has brought me into the reality again. I have what I need."

I looked up: there was not a man in the room who was not crying. The presence of the Lord was powerful among us.

Two nurses came to remind us that our time was up.

"Johnny," I said, "I'm going to see you on the other side."

"You can count on it!" he responded with a smile.

We filed out quietly, and headed south for Aurora. I don't know what it was like in the other cars but the five of us in my car spoke not a word.

Two days later Johnny Brighton died.

At the time, I had no idea of the extent of God's dealing in the hearts of those factory workers. As Johnny and I had fellowshipped together, oblivious to their presence, they had witnessed a graphic demonstration of Christian reality. They saw how a Christian man faces death. They saw the love of God flowing between two believers who scarcely knew each other. They saw that, in Christ, there can be hope and peace, even in the ultimate test, imminent death and leaving a young family behind. They felt the presence of Jesus and witnessed Him ministering to His own.

From that day forward, the door to the gospel was open at the factory. At first, I was greatly surprised, then the full realization of the opportunity and the responsibility hit home. My prayers were long and earnest that I might be a true witness to those people.

In the first couple of months at work, I was forthright about my faith in Christ, though not aggressive about it. Some of the men went out of their way to mock spiritual things when I was around. I tried to respond good-naturedly, and yet hold my ground.

One day I was operating a machine that applied a thin coating of wax to heavy paper. The foreman came by, "Do you know what this waxed paper will be used for?" he asked, raising his voice above the whirring of the machine.

"No, not exactly," I replied.

"It's a special order for Gooderham and Worts," he said with a sly grin, "You're making liners for whiskey bottle caps."

I made some adjustments to the machine, and then turned to him. "Well, Bill," I said, "G and W should be well pleased, because I'm turning out a good product here."

"I guess I can't argue with that," he retorted, then turned on his heel and left.

Tiny, a six foot nine, 325-pound giant drove the supply truck. Often when he passed my machine he would start singing an old hymn, "Leaning, leaning, leaning on the everlasting arms," I always smiled and said, "Thanks Tiny, that's a great song." On the other hand, sometimes I would sing along with him.

The man on the machine next to mine liked to make a mockery of the Scriptures. He would say things like, *"Many are called but few are chosen;* many are cold but few are frozen."

I just could not let it go by. "You may have to answer to God for that," I said once.

"I ain't worried," Steve said with a laugh.

After the visit we had with Johnny Brighton, all of these things came to an abrupt and complete halt. The men began to treat me with respect. Some came for spiritual help.

Bill, the foreman came to me one Monday morning, he was very upset. "Lee," he said, "please come into my office, I've got to talk to you."

I quickly followed him. He paced the floor. His eyes were bloodshot and tearful. "On Saturday night," he began, "my fourteen-year-old nephew was killed in a terrible car-crash east of town. He was a decent kid, brilliant in school; I loved him like my own son. Tell me, why would God do such a thing?"

"God didn't do that to your nephew, Bill," I returned. "Jesus came to bring life, abundant life, and eternal life. The devil came to steal, to kill, and to destroy. This world is corrupted by sin," I continued, "demonic powers are rampant and Satan is on the loose. Jesus is reaching out to us all in love and mercy, if we will only believe it and receive it."

I was able to help him to find peace and to pray for him.

I gave a tract to Steve at the next machine. "You take this pamphlet home," I instructed, "and tonight after you've got the kids to bed, you and your wife sit down and read this together. Read it over and over until you understand it; then do what it says, pray the prayer."

The next morning, after we had our machines set up and running, Steve was at my elbow. "Well, what about the tract?" I asked.

"My wife believes every word of it," he said, "And so do I. We prayed the prayer," he said.

I gave a tract, written by Evangelist, T.L.Osborn, to Hans, who had emigrated from Holland five years before. His face paled when he looked at it. "T.L.Osborn held a great crusade in Holland a few years ago," Hans said, "I attended many of the meetings. It was wonderful, thousands were saved and healed!"

"What about you, Hans?" I queried.

"I gave my heart to Jesus," he said, then he hung his head, "but something happened, I'm not following the Lord, now."

"He's calling you back today, Hans," I said softly, "this tract is a reminder, it's His calling card."

The next week a new man hired on. He was a well-built, good-looking young man of perhaps twenty. During the break time, he was standing behind a huge roll of paper talking to a group of men. As I walked past, I saw a vision. I was not experienced with such things and it startled me. In the vision, I saw this same young man, whom I had not yet met, dressed in a three-piece suit, the roll of paper became a pulpit and the young man was preaching to a crowd assembled before him.

I walked past the young man; as I came abreast of him I said quietly, "You're supposed to be preaching the gospel."

He was stunned, and ran after me. "Who are you? What do you know about me?" he whispered, hoarsely.

"I don't know a thing about you, young man," I returned, "but I saw a vision of you, well-dressed, standing behind a pulpit and preaching to a crowd."

"Oh Lord, Oh Lord, could it be?" he said, half to himself. The buzzer sounded, ending the break. "Can I talk to you?" he asked, almost pleading.

"Sure," I rejoined. I scribbled my address on a piece of paper. "Come over to my place after supper."

That night he told his story. His second year of Bible College was coming up in a couple of weeks, but something had happened. He felt he had failed God. "I didn't think He could use me, now," he explained, "so I got this job and decided to opt out of Bible College."

"The Lord doesn't seem to feel that way, does He?" I asked.

"Man, I'd do anything to get it right again," he said wistfully.

"Why not start with repentance?" I suggested, "And if there are things to be made right, make them right."

That young man was not fooling. He faced up to things and found the Lord had enough grace for him, too. I praised God that his career in the factory only lasted one day!

As I mentioned, the Lord had opened a door to the gospel in that factory. Many wonderful things happened in the few months I remained employed there. I pondered about it and wondered what the key was that unlocked such spiritual freedom in the place. Then I thought of Johnny Brighton and all those years of living for Jesus among those men, and all those years of praying for them, and finally, trusting the Lord as he faced death, before them. These are holy and precious things before God. Johnny's life, his prayers and his death, truly gave the Holy Spirit something to work with in unlocking the hearts of many.

CHAPTER 14

THE POWER OF HIS PRESENCE

It is precious and powerful when the Holy Spirit reveals that Jesus Christ is present. The presence of Christ is most difficult to define in human terms because it is of the Spirit, and is not merely of the intellect or the emotions.

The Holy Spirit may reveal Jesus Christ in us, as He did with the Apostle Paul, Galatians 1:15, 16. *"But when it pleased God who separated me from my mother's womb and called me through His grace, to reveal His Son in me..."*

He may reveal Christ to us, as Jesus, Himself said, John 15:21. *"and he that loves Me will be loved by My Father, and I will love him and manifest Myself to him."*

He may reveal the power of His presence with us, as He did in the early church, Mark 16:20. *"And they went out and preached everywhere, the Lord working with them and confirming the word through the accompanying signs."*

Of course, we Christians are called to walk by faith, not by sight. We do not need to see a vision, or to hear the Lord's voice booming to us from the heavens in order to find guidance. Nevertheless, the Lord is well able to reveal Himself powerfully and unmistakably, and when He does so, the impact is unforgettable.

In Aurora, Ontario, many years ago, I loaned my shovel to Louie Marshall. On the day, Louie and his family moved out of town, he discovered he had not returned my shovel. He phoned and said he would leave it with the landlady, who lived in the duplex downstairs.

That Saturday I called around to pick up my shovel. I noticed it leaning up against the wall by the back door.

I knocked and soon the landlady's son, a man in his mid-twenties, opened the door. I had heard a lot about this young man. He had several jail sentences behind him for theft, violence and alcohol offences. He told his friends that as a pastime he was attempting to see how many girls in the local high school he could get pregnant that year, at the time there were four. Young Brad was not the kind of a boy you would want living next door.

I stuck out my hand, "Hi Brad," I said, "I'm Lee. I just came to pick up my shovel."

As we shook hands, Brad became strangely agitated. His eyes widened and a look of fear, almost terror swept over his face. Then he broke into tears, got down on his knees before me on the back step and began to confess his sins. He was sobbing and almost incoherent as he went on and on confessing the evil and disgusting things, he had done in his evil and disgusting life.

The back door opened again, and Brad's mother, stepped out. The woman was grossly overweight and slatternly in appearance. A mop of unkempt, graying hair framed a coarse-featured, hard-looking countenance. The thought passed through my mind, Man, with a hag like this for a mother, no wonder Brad is like he is.

I held out my hand once more, "I'm Lee," I said, "I just came to get my shovel."

As soon as our hands touched, the woman was over-come by the same phenomenon that gripped her son. Wide-eyed and trembling in apparent fear, she knelt weeping beside her son on the concrete step, and poured out the sluttish history of her twisted life.

I stood silently, completely dumbfounded! I did not know what was happening, or why. I just stood there, not knowing what, if anything, I should be doing.

After a while, the two were silent and rose to their feet. They stared at me strangely and fearfully. I remained tongue-tied. The mother stepped quickly to the door and wrenched it open. Brad darted inside, glancing furtively over his shoulder at me. Then the woman herself lumbered quickly inside and slammed the door. I heard the lock click and then the dead bolt being rammed forcefully into place.

I finally snapped out of my befuddlement. Hey, I thought, these people are in desperate need of Jesus. They need to be saved. I should be helping them. I knocked at the door long and loudly and called out to them repeatedly. There was not a sound from inside. At last, I picked up my shovel and went home.

What really happened that afternoon? I am still not certain, but I have a sense that the Holy Spirit somehow revealed Christ in me–to them. From their fearful behavior and expressions, I can only conclude that it must have seemed to them that Jesus Himself, in all His holiness, was confronting them about the sinfulness of their lives.

About a year later, another young man named Craig came to our community. He was on parole from Kingston Penitentiary. Craig was a handsome young man in his late twenties, with dark eyes and jet-black hair. He was a tormented person filled with hatred and bitterness of soul. Craig bore such hatred against God and the church that he burned down a huge church building in Montreal, but not before urinating and defecating on the altar. Sadly, there were people in the building who lost their lives.

Craig's years in Dorchester and Kingston Penitentiaries inflamed his hatred to a new intensity.

Through his work in the Police Department, Jim Sleeth came to know Craig and his history. With a lot of patience and compassion, Jim tried to help the troubled man. "Only the love of Christ can heal a heart that's as crushed and wounded as his," Jim said. I got to know Craig through Jim, and had many talks with him about the Lord Jesus and the claims of the gospel.

Jim introduced Craig to the Christian community, and before long, He was seeing an attractive young girl from the Associated Gospel Church. We were very uneasy about it and warned the young woman about possible dangers in the relationship. I think she found it exciting to be going out with a handsome man who had a dark past.

Craig was lonely, and being with Susan seemed to raise faint hope that perhaps his life could change. He fell hard for the girl, but she did not have serious feelings for him, and eventually dumped him.

Craig could not handle it. Susan's rejection was like a pail of gasoline poured over the flame that seethed in his heart. It simply proved to him that he had been right all along about God, the church, and Christians and just about everybody else. His hatred broke out anew in every direction, and his life, driven by the old stirrings, spiraled downward to familiar depths. He started drinking again, and hung out with the criminal element in town. (Both parole violations).

One afternoon I received an urgent phone call from Jim Sleeth. "Craig has gone berserk!" he shouted into the phone. "I've just heard he's been drinking again and he's heading to your place to kill you, because you're always talking about Jesus."

"Don't worry, Jim," I replied, "I can handle a roomfull of guys like Craig."

"Maybe so," said Jim, "but be careful, he's nuts! Anyway, I'm coming right over."

I turned to the Lord immediately. "Lord, what's going to happen here?" I cried out, "This man needs You desperately, and yet I'm not going to put up with anything from him either. If he gets out of line, I'll put him on the floor."

The small, silent voice spoke sharply and clearly, in the heart of my spirit, "No, I don't want you to do anything but trust Me."

"But Jesus," I cried, "This is no time for the 'other cheek' stuff. This is serious! What if he kills me? What will happen to my family?"

"Trust Me," was the swift reply.

This was visceral praying, now. I tried to convince the Lord to listen to reason. His only response to everything was, "Trust Me."

At last, I surrendered. "All right, Lord," I said, "I will trust You, and I will not raise a hand to defend myself. Please help me to do it, Jesus."

That seemed to be a signal of some kind, for the door burst open and Craig stormed in. I was sitting on a work stool in my art-studio. The height of the stool raised me to the level of a man standing.

Craig was nuts all right! His face was flushed and mottled, his teeth barred, and an inhuman hatred blazed in his eyes. I remember thinking at the time, this man is demon-possessed!

With a stream of vile oaths, he ran at me.

I felt a very strange calm, and sat, arms folded.

The young ex-con swung at me four or five times, putting all his strength into every blow, but the punches never landed! At the last instant, each blow stopped, his fists less than a quarter inch from my face!

Craig stepped back about three paces. His face drained of color and a confused look came to his eyes. Then he seemed to get hold of himself and rushed again. This time he put his hands to my throat to choke me. Screaming curses, he tried repeatedly to position his hands, talon-like around my throat to strangle me. I could see him straining with all of his might to get hold of me, but he could not. His hands never touched me!

A look of absolute terror settled over his countenance, he uttered an unearthly scream and sank to his knees. He then slowly sagged forward, and with his face on the floor, he wept in a hopeless kind of way, his body wracked by pain-filled sobs. The pathos of that scene haunts me still.

Jim Sleeth shuffled in, moving purposefully despite his handicap. He looked at the stricken Craig, then looked questioningly at me.

I shrugged. I did not understand it either. "This man needs deliverance, Jim," I said, "I believe he's demon-possessed."

Jim nodded. We laid hands on the troubled man and earnestly prayed. We spoke in the authority of the name of

Jesus, and sought to break the powers of the dark world. Craig became very subdued and rational, but we were not at all satisfied that he had been truly set free. He would not make a decision to put his trust in the Lord.

"I've got to take you back to the station, Craig," Jim said. "You've broken parole a dozen ways."

The young man nodded. "I know," he said softly.

I pleaded with him to give his heart to Jesus; He looked at me with blank eyes, and raised his hands, palms up, then let them fall to his sides in resignation. He hung his head and walked out to the van with Jim.

Craig returned to Kingston Pen to serve out his sentence. Jim told me later that as he drove the young man back to the Police Station, Craig said, "I was never so scared in my life! That Lee has God with him. I hit him four or five times as hard as I could but it never touched him. I tried and tried to strangle him, but there is an invisible shield around him. I could not get my hands on his throat. He has God all around him!"

Maybe being, *"in Christ"* as the Bible says, is more literal than we think.

CHAPTER 15

SPREADING THE WORD ON YONGE

Many people have made a commitment to Jesus Christ through reading gospel literature. An effective method of distributing the printed message of salvation is through gospel tracts or small pamphlets.

Throughout my Christian life, I have handed out tracts. Earlier on, I was very zealous about it. I ordered tracts by the thousand and distributed them on the streets of Toronto.

Eventually our family moved from Ontario to my home-province, Saskatchewan. The week before the move, I discovered I had nearly a thousand tracts on hand, all bearing the stamp of our Willowdale Pentecostal Church.

That Saturday, I parked near Yonge and Bloor, shopped for some last-minute art supplies at Curies Art Store, and set out to distribute a giant stock of tracts. It looked like an insurmountable task but I was praying fervently for the Lord's help.

I crossed to the east side of Yonge Street, at Bloor, and walked down the center of the sidewalk so I could hand out literature to people on both sides.

The first person I met was a big police officer. I quickly extended a tract. He never broke stride, but fixing me with an expressionless stare, he accepted the piece, nodded thanks and slipped it into the pocket of his tunic.

The next recipient was a young sign painter working on a store window. "Well praise the Lord, it's the gospel isn't it?" he asked with a toothy grin.

"It is," I responded.

"Well, would you be a Christian yourself?" he queried.

"Yes I am," I replied.

"And would you happen to be a Pentecostal believer, then?" the toothy man asked.

"Yeah, I'm that, too," I returned.

"Hallelujah!" the man exalted. "I'm a Pentecostal Christian myself, from Saint Johns, Newfoundland."

We had a few minutes of fellowship and I was greatly encouraged. This is a great way to start! I thought.

Sidewalk traffic increased steadily as I proceeded slowly south on Yonge. Some refused the literature of course, but most received it. After nearly an hour, I was still above Dundas Street. I had decided I would turn around there and head back. It was disappointing to see, by the huge wad of tracts that remained, that I would not even distribute half of them in the roughly two hours I still had available.

At that point, something changed, abruptly. The change was even physically discernable, as though the atmospheric pressure or some other measurable force had altered. Though it was a beautiful sunny afternoon, it felt as though a fog that had never been there suddenly lifted. Everything was different; the people were different, I was different. I stood still and waited to see what would happen.

I did not have long to wait...suddenly people seemed to notice me. I didn't move after that; the people came to me! I handed out tracts as fast as I could. People were eager; they stood in line to get the word of God!

By now, a crowd was gathering that spilled out into the street. Car traffic was at a crawl, and soon came to a halt. People crossed the street from the west side of Yonge. Though a lot was happening, everything was quiet and orderly.

A young man said, "Give me some of them and I'll hand them out down the street." I gave him several dozen tracts. He said to his friend, "You take some and go up that way." I gave him a handful, too.

I heard a man in a car shout, "We need four!" Another said, "Can we have three, here?"

It was uncanny! Incredible! People were taking a number of tracts and handing them out to perfect strangers around them. Hundreds of tracts were distributed in a very short time. I confess I do not know what happened to us all out there on Yonge Street that afternoon. However, most certainly it was something the Lord, Himself accomplished.

I glanced down the street toward Dundas just as two policemen sprinted around the corner, batons in hand. I am sure they thought a serious altercation of some kind was in progress. Traffic on Yonge Street was at a standstill and several hundred people filled the sidewalk and street.

Just as the officers approached the fringe of the crowd, I handed out the last tract. That seemed to be a signal; everything that had changed so remarkably that short while before, softly, but very definitely changed back. Immediately, I was no longer a center of attention, but just one of the onlookers. The crowd dispersed quickly and in an orderly manner. Car traffic resumed its flow.

The two officers were confused. "What just happened here?" I heard them ask several people. I saw them shrug and walk on. Well, I thought, if they ask me, I guess I really do not have a good explanation either.

As I walked back north toward Bloor Street I prayed, "Lord, I don't know what You did back there, or how You did it, but, thank You! Thank You! Thank You! That is the most astounding thing I have ever witnessed!

I had the idea at the time that the Lord was smiling, perhaps even chuckling. After all, "Is anything too hard for the Lord?"

CHAPTER 16

WILDERNESS TRAPLINE

This is an excerpt from a chapter in my book, *"Edge Of The Wilderness, growing up in the north,"* Fifth House Publishers, 2004. It was written of a time in my youth before I became a Christian. I have included it here to illustrate the mercy and grace of God, even toward those who do not know or serve Him.

He has this degree of love for us all! Romans 5:8 *"God demonstrated His love for us in that while we were yet sinners, Christ died for us."*

A wilderness trapline can be a great place to discover what kind of stuff you are truly made of, especially if you are alone and sixteen. I ran such a trapline by myself during the early season of 1948. I had almost more than I could handle of excitement, danger, and plain hard work.

That experience had a strong influence on my life. Though many years have since passed, recollections of the north country remain vivid.

Late in my second week at Stinking Lake, I embarked on an all-day journey to explore Falling Horse and Caribou Creeks. Fred had given me a roughly penciled map, and I knew the streams ran parallel. I planned to scout for animal sign and return to set traps where prospects were best. I traveled five or six miles, following the map to the Falling Horse. It looked promising, but I pressed on a few more miles to a larger stream that I correctly assumed was Caribou Creek.

A couple of moose had recently passed that way so I did not bother to test the ice. I slid down the six-foot bank and started across.

Without warning, the ice crumbled before me and was swept away by swift, black water. As the footing gave way, I flipped my rifle across the creek and lunged forward with everything I had. I managed to grab the tips of some branches of a huge poplar the beavers had felled into the creek from the opposite bank. It seemed my pack, belt-axe and sodden clothing weighed a ton. The current pulled with relentless force as though set on my demise. At that moment, those flimsy, frozen branches were the difference between life and death. Miraculously the branches held. Hand over hand I hauled myself toward the tree. It seemed to take forever to find the trunk with my feet, deep under water. Finally, I began gingerly to climb up the slope of the huge trunk.

I had never before experienced anything as cold as the black waters of the Caribou. However, I definitely was not prepared for the jolt that came next. As I emerged from the water, soaked to the skin, a stiff breeze and twenty below zero air temperature hit with the force of an avalanche! Searing, paralyzing cold penetrated to my very bones. I wanted to give up, but somehow kept crawling. Finally, I toppled into the snow on the far bank.

After several attempts, I lurched to my feet. Although my body was almost immobile, my mind worked feverishly. My first thought was to get a fire going. Then I made an astonishing discovery...I wasn't so cold anymore. I wondered if I was hallucinating, or perhaps entering a new stage of coldness where feeling malfunctioned. Then, I looked down at my clothes and saw I was wearing a suit of armor–ice armor! The extreme cold had flash-frozen my outer garments, sealing out the cold and trapping my body heat inside.

I dropped the idea of trying to build a fire. Instead, I rescued my rifle from the snow bank and struck out for camp at a brisk pace.

The trip back to camp was not without challenge, but neither was it unbearable. In fact, I was surprisingly comfortable. I thought about a good fire in the airtight heater, and a hefty pot of grouse stew.

I had no real concept of God in those days, but I had a deep sense as I trudged along that more than luck had spared my life. I was thankful.

A short time after my expedition to the Caribou, I was awakened about mid-night one night by a sound, like no other–the plaintive howl of a northern timber wolf. Soon there was another, then another, then a full chorus. I slid deeper into the eiderdown sleeping bag and soon dozed off.

Louder howling quickly had me wide awake. It was closer this time, up on the jack pine ridge west of camp, I guessed.

I got up, lit the coal-oil lamp and fed a couple of chunks of dry pine into the airtight. Intermittent howling came steadily closer. "Hey," I declared aloud, "they're heading right for this cabin!"

I tried to reassure myself by recalling everything I had heard or read, to the effect that wolves are afraid of humans. Somehow, it provided little comfort when I heard the next mournful, chilling cry not thirty feet from the cabin door.

I grabbed my 25-20 carbine, levered a round into the chamber and sat down on the bunk. By now, I could hear wolves moving through the snow in the dry weeds and brush.

Although it was cool inside, my palms were sweating as I gripped the cold steel. I kept my eyes on the window in the west wall. It was low enough and large enough for a wolf to jump through. The window had no glass but was covered on the inside with a sheet of semi-transparent waxed cloth. It would be foolish to think that a wolf would rip through that cloth and leap into an occupied cabin, wouldn't it? I was not so sure anymore, as I heard shaggy fur brush against the rough pine bark of the logs under the window. The hair on the back of my neck stood up. I cocked the carbine and waited…

CHAPTER 17

LORD OF THE WEATHER

For many years I ran, almost every day. I enjoyed being in good shape and running is a great conditioner. In recent years, I have scaled back from running ten miles to a brisk daily walk of about three miles.

One day in late May, I set out under a heavily overcast sky. Soon the wind picked up and with it came a serious cloudburst. I was getting soaked! I sprinted for shelter under a huge maple just off the sidewalk. I was well protected, but temporarily trapped. I could not proceed with my walk, neither could I call it off nor head home. The rain slanted down furiously, driven by a now chilling wind. Already large puddles were forming in the street, their surfaces churned and riddled by the relentless raindrops.

As I took stock of the situation, I became annoyed and impatient. An aggressive thought came...I peered out into the pelting downpour and spoke aloud, "In the name of Jesus, stop!" Instantly, it did! I looked at the, now large puddles; the surface of every one of them was mirror-like and undisturbed. The rain didn't taper off gradually, it just stopped, totally and instantly! I stood slack-jawed and amazed as the realization of what had just happened sank in. I quickly began to thank the Lord and to praise Him for His kindness.

I resumed my walk but now found that my jacket was soaked through and I was getting downright cold. I felt a little selfish, nevertheless I prayed again, more thoughtfully this time. "Lord," I said, "You have so graciously stopped the rain, now can You help me overcome the cold?" In five minutes the cloud cover separated, the wind stopped and the sun came out. I was soon very comfortable and by the time I reached home, my jacket was completely dry.

I felt very humbled and close to Jesus that day. Truly, that was a miracle walk, a walk to remember.

Whenever the Lord does a special or a miraculous thing for us, it is not so much the miracle He has done that touches us deeply, but rather the fresh demonstration that He knows where we are and what we face, and that He is with us, even in the daily affairs of life.

This miracle walk was not the only time the Lord has intervened on my behalf during a rainstorm. In the early 1970s, I worked as an advertising sales rep for Otto Janzen, owner and publisher of the Nipawin Journal, North East Community Booster and several other publications, in northern Saskatchewan. One morning I left Nipawin on a sales trip to Melfort, a small, nearby city. The sky was threatening and before I was halfway there, the rain was so heavy the wipers could barely keep the windshield clear. I prayed that it would stop; it only seemed to get worse. As I neared Melfort, my concern increased for I had no raincoat and I did not relish spending the day trying to successfully represent our publications, wearing sodden clothing.

The first business I called on was a large R.V. dealer-ship on the outskirts of town. I pulled up in front, still the rain pounded down relentlessly. I waited for a while, hoping for a let-up, which did not happen. At last, I decided to trust God and get on with it. I asked for His help, but had no idea how He could provide it. I grabbed my briefcase, hustled the 30 or 40 feet to the front door, and stepped inside, quickly.

The manager and several salesmen watched, grinning broadly, expecting that I would resemble a drowned rat.

The manager stepped closer to shake hands, "You must be soak...ed..." His voice trailed off. I did a double take myself when I looked down and found I was absolutely dry! There was not even a drop of rain on my briefcase! The man went to the door, opened it and saw the rain still streaming down furiously. "How come you're not wet?" he blurted out.

"Well Joe," I replied, "I prayed and I guess the Lord kept me dry."

"Whew!" he whistled through his teeth, "Whew!" Joe looked nervous, and a little pale. I, however, felt very confident. Talk about a sales advantage!

It rained all day in Melfort, but not a drop touched me. I know this sounds like a fanciful, made-up story, but it is true. I had a full day of selling, calling on more than 20 clients. Every time some astonished person asked how I could walk in out of the pouring rain and be dry, I told them, "I'm trusting Jesus and this is something He's doing for me today." Ad sales that day in Melfort were very, very good.

On the way back to Nipawin the rain began to ease. Before I pulled into town, it had stopped. Otto greeted me as I stepped into the office. "Bet you got soaked," he said, then, "Wait a minute, you don't look wet at all." He touched my jacket. "Dry as a bone," he said, "How come?"

"Otto," I replied, "I can't believe how gracious the Lord has been to me today. It rained all day in Melfort, it just didn't rain on me."

"Wow!" he exclaimed, "That's a wonderful thing!"

"I know it," I responded. "I'm rejoicing, but at the same time I feel very humble, too."

"I can understand that," Otto rejoined, "and I'm happy for you, but I have to confess I wish it had happened to me."

In August of 1970, the congregation of the Pentecostal Church in the village of White Fox in northern Saskatchewan officially got under way with the construction of a new church. Reverend Carson Latimer was the pastor and the contractor they hired to oversee construction was a godly man from Melfort, named Mike Panchuk. They hired one paid construction worker, me. Most of the rest of the labor force were folks from the congregation who worked on a volunteer basis.

Our family had moved from Toronto the previous summer. The winter that followed was unusually mild, and I did not have adequate winter clothing for a normal Saskatchewan winter.

As work on the church progressed into late October the fall weather was very strange; balmy days almost alternated with unseasonably cold spells. I was wearing a Toronto jacket the November day winter set in for good. It was cold in the morning and grew steadily worse. As the mercury plummeted a wicked north wind seared across Bill Kingsley's stubble field, punishing our unprotected workplace. The other workers had heavy coats and parkas, and while they were feeling the cold, I was freezing. I hunched against the wind and worked at a frenzied pace in order to keep my circulation at a high level. At about eleven o'clock, I doubted that I could survive it much longer. I ducked out of the wind behind the construction shed and prayed, "Lord Jesus, I'm giving it all I've got but I don't think I can make it through the afternoon. Please help me." I am not a great believer of hearing voices, but something deep inside of me spoke. It was not an audible voice but it was a distinct and clear communication. He, and I believe it was the Spirit of Christ, said, "I am going to cover you. From now on you will be warm." Immediately I felt a warm covering from head to foot, like a toasty-warm electric blanket. The wind howled as before but now it did not touch me. I know the bitter, below-zero temperature had not changed but surrounding me was the warmth of a summer day. I couldn't understand it but I enjoyed it with every living cell in my body, and I shouted my thanks to Jesus into the teeth of that merciless Saskatchewan wind. I relaxed and worked at a normal pace, no longer hunching my shoulders against the wind because though its force was undiminished, I could not feel it. It crossed my mind that perhaps I was hallucinating and had passed into some kind of a numbness stage of being cold, but no, I knew it was real, and I knew it was Jesus, and He was keeping His word.

Mike Panchuk was aware of my situation. He said, "You should go home for lunch now and don't come back today. You're going to kill yourself out here."

"No Mike, I'm warm now, it's okay," I responded.

"That's absurd!" he replied, "Nobody can face a day like this in the clothes you're wearing."

"Its okay, Mike," I assured him, "I prayed and Jesus answered, right here," I said, tapping my chest. "He said He would cover me and that I would be warm, and He has, the wind doesn't even touch me."

"Praise the Lord!" Mike exulted, "That's a marvelous thing! I've never seen anything like it!"

We worked through the day. I have a hunch I was the most comfortable man on the crew. When the Lord does a job, it is never second best.

About four in the afternoon Pastor Latimer's car pulled up to the building site. He motioned me over. "Get in the back seat," he said, "I've got something for you."

I climbed in the back seat and there was a beautiful khaki parka, arctic issue. "Wow! That's a beauty!" I exclaimed.

"Yeah, well it's yours," he said. "I saw you freezing out here this morning in that big-city jacket. I have another parka and I haven't worn this one in years."

"I'm actually not freezing anymore," I explained, "The Lord is keeping me warm."

"I'm glad He is," the pastor replied, "but He spoke to me, too, and you're supposed to have this parka." He seemed a little gruff about it and was in a hurry. I thanked him and went back to work in a tremendous parka.

That was 36 years ago. Moreover, here is a strange add-on to that story of God's kindness and grace all those years ago. Recently, long retired, Reverend Carson Latimer and I were having coffee at a Tim Horton's in Edmonton; we talked about that cold day in White Fox when he gave me the parka.

"You know I didn't want to give you that parka," he said. "You see, for years I worked as a Federal Fisheries

Officer in the far north. After I became a Christian and later went into ministry, I saved that parka as a memento of an exciting time in my life as a young man in the North West Territories. When I drove by the building site and saw you trying to keep from freezing, and I knew you didn't have the money to buy a decent parka, the Lord spoke clearly to me and said, 'Give that man your arctic parka.' I argued with the Lord. I did not want to do it. I finally gave in, but at the time I wasn't happy about it."

We had a good laugh, and praised the Christ who can still speak into the hearts of His people, and knows when it's best for us to give something, and when it's best to receive something.

Personally, I am glad the Lord stepped in with His covering, until His servant was ready to part with his.

CHAPTER 18

STARTING OVER WITH JESUS

In 1970, our family lived in the village of White Fox, Saskatchewan, during the construction of the new Pentecostal Church there. I was the only paid laborer working with contractor, Mike Panchuk and a crew of volunteer workers.

The wage I received was not quite adequate to meet the needs of our family. My wife, Beverly and I prayed about our finances, earnestly. Finally, in early December we realized it was time to do something about it. The bills were mounting, the children needed clothes and Christmas was coming. We decided that I should go to Prince Albert and borrow about four hundred and fifty dollars from a finance company to tide us over until the building project was completed. I planned then to get a better paying job in Nipawin. Borrowing money did not seem to us to be the Lord's way, but it was a way, and immediate action was necessary.

The next day I headed for the city of Prince Albert, about 85 miles to the southwest. I located the finance company on Central Avenue and walked in. All the staff was occupied with clients, but almost immediately, a well-dressed young man stepped out of his office to greet me. He looked to be perhaps twenty-five, very confident, friendly and professional in his demeanor. He introduced himself as the Branch Manager and invited me to have a seat in his office. I noticed his office was expensively furnished. The young man asked how he could be of help.

I explained my situation and my desire to secure a loan for four hundred and fifty dollars. I mentioned that I had a credit history with a branch of his company in west-Toronto.

He made a quick phone call, and then turning to me with a ready smile he said, "Man, you have a gilt edged credit record with our company. I'll be happy to provide whatever you need, and I'll get it done right now."

He prepared the necessary documents, as one who obviously had done it a thousand times. He extended the papers across the desk for my signature, and stepped out of the room for a few minutes. When he returned, he separated the documents, placing my copies neatly before me. Then, producing an envelope from an inside pocket, proceeded to count out four hundred and fifty dollars in crisp, new bills. He stacked them neatly beside the loan documents.

I was impressed. "I've never had better service," I remarked, "it took me nearly two hours to drive down here, and I haven't been in your office fifteen minutes and the deal is done!"

The young manager grinned broadly and sat back in his classy leather chair. "That's how we do business here," he said.

It was time to shake hands and leave but something was stirring in me. I sensed the Holy Spirit wanted something said; I was not sure what it was. I took a deep breath and began to speak carefully, sort of feeling my way. "You know Frank," I began, "I am a believer in the Lord Jesus Christ. I came to know Jesus personally about eight years ago, and since that time He has guided me, protected me, and met my needs many times. In fact, I really don't think I need to be here borrowing money from you. This makes me question the real purpose of my being here, and makes me suspect that I have been sent here by God for some other reason." I gestured toward the money. "You have been used to meet my financial need," I observed. "I believe I have been sent here by God so that He can meet your need, whatever that may be."

What happened next was so astonishing I did not know what to say, so I said nothing, I simply watched in amazement, as that suave, self-assured, young business manager became another person, in countenance, in demeanor, in posture. It was like a weird theatrical performance by some gifted thespian. Gone were the easy confidence, the professional manner, and the engaging smile. There was no attempt to maintain composure, he stared vacantly, his lips trembled, and his face was as white as the loan documents he had so deftly prepared. I wondered if he was having a seizure of some kind.

Finally, he gasped out of seemingly parched lips, "Man, I just can't believe this! Man, I just can't believe this!"

I still had nothing to say. (This was probably wisdom by default).

The man struggled to get control of himself, he took a couple of deep breaths and his voice took on a more normal tone as he said again, "Man, I just can't believe this! And I don't think you'll be able to, either."

"Try me," I replied, "I have a hunch I will."

"To most people it looks like I'm a guy who has it all," he began, "I'm a branch manager at twenty four, I make great money, I'm respected in the community, I drive a BMW, and I take trips to places like Vegas and New York. But inside, the things that really matter are in shambles!" He was crying openly now, "There's a relationship that's broken and it can never be recovered," he cried, "and I just can't get past it. Other personal matters are so out of control I just can't come to peace with myself."

"Late last night I drove out of town and parked on a hill," he continued. He opened the top right hand drawer of his desk and brought out a nickel-plated, short-barreled revolver. "I took my .38 along," he said. He twirled the cylinder several times; it made a soft clicking sound. I could see that every chamber was loaded. After what seemed a long time he restored the weapon to the drawer. "I went out of town last night," Frank said, "and I didn't intend to come back. I cocked the .38, but something inside of me, or in the car said, 'Wait.'

"I put the gun down and I cried for a long time, I just couldn't stop. When I finally couldn't cry any more I looked out the windshield. It was clear last night and the stars looked so bright, so close, and so real. I started to wonder if there was a God after all. I never believed God existed. I never looked for Him, and He sure never came looking for me." he confided, "But the thought of God wouldn't go away. Finally, I talked toward God, out toward the stars. I said, 'God, if You exist, if You're really out there, If You can hear me, and if You care about me, I'm giving You one more day to prove it. I'm asking You to send somebody to help me tomorrow. Moreover, I have to be sure You sent him. If You don't do it, I'll be back out here tomorrow night with this .38, because I'll know either You're not there, or You just don't care."

Frank was getting control of himself again and he was very intense. I knew he was thinking about the remarks I had made earlier about the Lord.

"My God!" he exploded, "You said you were sent here by God to help me. Is all of this real?"

"What does it look like to you?" I asked quietly.

"My God, I think it is real!" he exclaimed. A shiver went through his body. Tears were flowing again.

Now it was my time to talk. "Frank," I said, "this is a life and death matter. You did the right thing; you took it to God, Himself. Maybe you do not realize it but you prayed out there on the hill last night. You talked to God. You challenged Him to prove himself, and He has done it. He sent me here today. I'm a man sent from God, to you, in answer to your prayer."

"Man!" he said, "I can't believe this, but I do believe it! You're coming here today and saying those things could never happen by chance in a million years!"

"But can you help me?" his words were pleading, almost desperate, "Can this Jesus you believe in, help me?"

I felt very confident. "Frank," I said, "the Christ who loved you enough to hear your prayer last night, who loved you enough to answer your prayer today, has power to give you everything you need right here, right now!"

I don't know if I have ever met anyone who was more eager to hear the gospel than this man was. I read some scriptures from my pocket Testament, and explained the truths about sin, the love of God, the death and resurrection of Jesus, repentance and 'by grace through faith.' He needed no coaching in prayer. His repentance was tearful and forthright, and his faith seemed to take hold immediately.

Almost everything was as it was. I still sat in the comfortable, leather client's chair, the lavish décor of the manager's office remained the same, and the neat stack of new bills was still positioned meticulously beside the loan documents; but for the second time that afternoon the man in the manager's chair had passed through a dramatic transformation. Young Frank sat erectly now, his face beamed, as from some secret interior illumination. He smiled broadly, not the cocksure, practiced smile of a business professional, but a genuine smile from a genuine human being.

"Well...ah... sorry I've forgotten your name," he said.

"Lee," I supplied.

"Yeah, yeah, Lee," he continued, "I have a feeling I've never had before, right here," he placed a hand on the center of his chest, "Is this what it feels like to have Jesus in your heart?"

"It is," I replied. "The intensity of that feeling will come and go but He will never leave you,"

"I know it! I believe it!" Frank asserted. "When I think of everything that has happened in the last twenty four hours and realize He did it all for me... I know He loves me, I know He is with me; I know he has power for anything. And all this stuff that I can't handle," he went on, "It's going to work out, I don't know how, but when it does it's going to be Jesus."

93

The manager was thoughtful for a moment. "You know my older brother, Al in Hamilton, tried to talk to me about God," he said, "I never believed there was a God so I wouldn't listen to him."

"Your brother is a Christian?" I queried.

"Yes," he replied, "he and his family attend church all the time and he talks about Jesus like you do."

"I've got to go now," I said, "but I want you to call your brother today. Tell him everything that has happened here, and give me a call soon. I want to know how you're doing."

Frank agreed, we had a brief prayer; I gave him my Testament and was soon heading north and east on Highway 55 toward White Fox.

Three days later Frank called. "I phoned Al," he said, "Boy was he excited to hear that I've accepted Jesus! Here is some more news; I have quit the company. I am going home to Hamilton next week. I'll be staying at Al's until I find a place. He is going to help me connect with a good church. You told me God made me a new man. Well the new man is starting over with a new life, only this time he's starting out with Jesus!"

CHAPTER 19

DESPERATION

It was shortly after eleven, Saturday morning when the phone rang; we were living in the village of White Fox, Saskatchewan at the time. The caller was Jean, Pastor Latimer's wife. She was crying and very distraught. "Lee, she said, "Please come over and help us, Carson is terribly sick. There has been a multi-vehicle crash south of Nipawin, and all the doctors are unavailable. There's no ambulance free to come, either," she cried, "I don't know what to do." I could hear her husband's agonized screams in the background.

"Okay, I'll be right over," I answered. I grabbed a jacket and tore out of the house on the run.

It is amazing how what begins as an ordinary day, can suddenly become a scene of desperation. Those folks on Highway 35, south of Nipawin were thrust unexpectedly into a desperate situation by a terrible accident. Pastor Latimer was in a desperate situation because of his illness. His wife was in a desperate state because she did not know how to get help for him. Now, as I pounded up that alley at full speed, I was desperate! I had seen God heal sick people in answer to prayer. The Lord had even used me to help others many times, but somehow this was different. My faith had unexplainably leaked away somewhere and I was plainly scared to go where I was going. The irony of it was that I was running as fast as I could, to get where I did not want to go.

Finally, I slowed to a walk, and stopped. "Lord," I cried, "this is my pastor. He is the man of God. He's the one who helps people. He prays for the sick. What can I do? Lord, I just don't want to go there."

There was no answer and I immediately felt ashamed of my fear, but no less empty and helpless. I cried to the Lord again, even more desperately this time, "Jesus, please give me something to go with, I feel so helpless like this."

Immediately, I heard it; a line from a hymn being sung by a church congregation... somewhere. How could this be possible? I thought. There are no churches nearby. It was an early fall day, overcast, chilly, and very windy. Nevertheless, the words of that hymn were so distinct. Every word was perfectly clear. I wondered if this was God.

"Jesus," I prayed, "if that came from You, please do it again."

Instantly, the same line from the same hymn rang out with perfect clarity.

"Thank You Jesus," I whispered, and was running flat-out again in a moment.

I slowed to a trot when I was about a block from the house. The pastor's screams cut through the wind like a rusty saw-blade and unnerved me, for I knew him to be a strong, tough man.

I pushed open the back door and stepped into the kitchen. Jean stood near the sink, head bowed, weeping. "He's in there," she whispered tearfully, motioning toward the bedroom.

The scene in the bedroom rocked me to the very core. Carson, my pastor and friend, lay fully clothed on the bed, threshing and writhing in pain. He slobbered, and his face was puffy and mottled. He stared with sightless eyes, moaning and crying out in obvious agony.

I was so rattled I think I was in a state of shock myself. I forgot about the words of the hymn. I cried out to the Lord in prayer. I laid hands on the stricken man. I rebuked the devil. Nothing changed! Carson, in his delirium, was oblivious to my presence. It seemed like the Lord was absent, too.

Shaken and discouraged I sat on a chair at the head of the bed. Carson continued in his distress. My heart was broken over his need that remained unmet.

Suddenly the silent voice spoke again, "Use what I gave you," it said.

Yes, the hymn! I remembered it now. Those few words were as clear as if they had been burned into my brain. I did not think I was to sing them, so I just spoke them quietly and matter-of-factly, to no one in particular.

Immediately, there was complete stillness and silence on the bed. Carson drew a deep breath, "Hallelujah!" he announced with a loud voice "Praise the Lord that's over!" His eyes were clear, his face was of normal color and there was no slobber. Still unaware of my presence, he swung his legs over and sat up. "Lee," he said in surprise, "What are you doing here?"

I was so overwhelmed by, first, the trauma of things as they were, then by the power of the miracle that had just unfolded, that I was speechless. Finally, I mumbled, "Well, ah…I just stopped by…guess I'll be going now." With that, I left.

Strangely, I never discussed that incident with Carson Latimer until 30 years later. He was very surprised about it all. "I have no recollection of any of that," he said, "All I remember is that I was desperately sick and in unbelievable pain. I lay down on the bed and everything sort of faded out. Then I woke up feeling well, great in fact, and you were sitting there."

How like Jesus to use the words of a hymn to release the healing power His servant desperately needed. My part was simply to deliver the message. However, isn't that what ministry really is, after all?

CHAPTER 20

WHO'S PAYING THE BILL?

A small group of us worked steadily through the fall and winter of 1970/71 constructing the Pentecostal Church in White Fox, Saskatchewan. Except for Mike Panchuk, the contractor, and me, the workers were volunteers.

Old Pop Macgregor showed up for work almost every day. Because of his age, Pop could do very little work but he enjoyed sharing in the fellowship at the building site. Mike always made sure he had a little job of some kind for the old fellow to tinker at.

One day Mike announced, "What this outfit needs is a designated tea-maker. Anybody want to take on the responsibility?"

"I think I can handle 'er, Mike," the old man responded quickly. Thereafter, Pop MacGregor became the official break-time, tea-maker for the construction crew. For the time, it gave him a sense of purpose that had been missing in his life for some years. He took the job seriously and hardly ever missed a day. Though Pop was not strong, we noticed that many times his tea certainly was!

In late winter, we finished the new church building and dedicated it on Good Friday, 1971. Almost immediately, I began working for Otto Janzen in Nipawin as an advertising rep. for several of his publications. One afternoon I met Pop MacGregor on Main Street in Nipawin. He looked haggard and very down in the mouth. I tried to cheer him up but he remained glum.

"I haven't had a good cup of tea since we finished the building in White Fox," I said, "Let's stop in at the Welcome Café and have tea." MacGregor perked up a little and we went in. We had tea and some of Bing's raisin pie. We joked around for a while and then began to talk about the goodness of the Lord. Pop shared about his loneliness and discouragement, and we prayed there in the booth. Soon Pop was "himself" again and we had a good visit.

Suddenly a horrible realization came to me; I remembered that I had forgotten my wallet in my other pants and I did not have a red cent on me! I had invited this lonely old man to the restaurant to encourage him, and now I was going to stick him with the bill!

I cried out to the Lord, fervently, in my heart. "Lord, show me what to do. Forgive my thoughtlessness and help me please!"

The front door swung open and Henry, the proprietor of a dry cleaning business down the street sauntered in. He came over to our booth. "Hi Lee," he said, "having coffee?"

"No, tea," I replied.

"Tea," he rejoined, "I haven't had tea for a heck of a long time. Mind if I join you?"

"Glad to have you," I said, "Have a seat."

Bing brought tea for Henry and dropped the bills for both of us on our table. I introduced the two men and we chatted amiably for a few minutes.

The door opened again and another local businessman entered. "Hey," said Henry quickly, "I've got to talk to that guy." He rose and picked up his tea mug, "It's been good talking to you guys; and I'll take care of this," he said over his shoulder as he scooped up his bill, and mine.

CHAPTER 21

FRIENDS AND RELATIVES

I got the bad news about my cousin Mervin by phone one evening. "Cancer," they said, "liver cancer." He was receiving chemotherapy though, and those close to him were hopeful.

I was really shaken. I thought a lot of my cousin, He was a big, strong man in his early forties, It just did not seem right.

In a while, I found out that apparently results from the chemo were favorable, and Merv was anxious to get back to work.

Then more bad news, Merv's condition was steadily worsening. A week later, my Mom called; Merv was dead.

I made the 400-mile trip home for the funeral and berated myself most of the way for not traveling back while he was yet alive. I could have prayed for him. I should have prayed for him.

I remembered that many years earlier, I was overcome by noxious fumes while climbing out of a 50-foot well. Merv saved my life that day.

At age 32, I had a life-changing encounter with the Lord Jesus Christ. I talked to Merv at great length about it, and urged him to receive Christ as I had done. He deferred, saying he believed the gospel was true, but felt he was not ready to make such a commitment. As I drove up Highway 35 into northern Saskatchewan, I had no idea if Merv had ever given his heart to Christ. I was not at peace.

When I reached my parent's home in Nipawin, the first thing I asked Mom was, "Do you know if Mervin was a saved man?"

"Oh, yes," Mom replied, "he certainly was!"

I rejoiced and praised God, then asked Mom how it came about. She told me the amazing story.

A short time before his death, Merv became much weaker. He was in and out of hospital, but preferred to stay at home. He had a hospital bed set up in his home in the village of Love.

Knowing that Merv was not a Christian and was near death, caused Mom grave concern. One night she wept in prayer for hours about it. She asked the Lord to reveal Himself to Merv in a dream that would help him to surrender and believe.

That night Merv was rocked by a frightening dream. In it, he saw himself helpless on the bed. Suddenly a man in white clothing appeared at the foot of the bed. The man had long, black hair and a beard. He had kind eyes, and He smiled and beckoned to Merv to come near. My cousin tried desperately to comply but was too feeble to do so. At last, the man left.

At this point, Merv woke up in a cold sweat. He knew this was different from any dream he had ever had, and he was greatly distressed.

Despite the fact that it was in the early hours of the morning, Mervin immediately called his close friend, Bill. He described the dream to his friend and explained that he felt there was a spiritual connotation involved that he could not understand. "Bill, you're a Christian," he said, "You've attended church. Please come over and help me understand the meaning of this dream."

Bill said no, that he could not come immediately, but perhaps he would come later.

Merv, confused by this, pleaded with his friend for help.

The man said he would come as soon as he could, and hung up.

Mervin spent a sleepless night. First thing in the morning, however, his friend, Bill showed up. "I've done a lot of praying, Merv," he said, "I'm sorry I couldn't come earlier but my own life was not right with the Lord. I am so thankful He has forgiven and restored me; now I can help you.

"I believe this is the meaning of the dream, the man you saw was Jesus. He's calling you to come to Him, but you can't come because you're not a Christian."

"I know I'm not a Christian," said Merv, earnestly, "I heard about it years ago, but I never did accept Jesus as my Savior. Will you help me, Bill?"

The two friends prayed and that morning, Mervin received the Lord Jesus Christ into his heart.

In a few weeks my cousin, Mervin answered the call of that Man in white clothing, and went to be with him for eternity.

CHAPTER 22

VENGEANCE IS MINE

After the construction of Hi-Way Tabernacle in White Fox, Saskatchewan was completed; I needed a job. Otto Janzen, owner/publisher of the Nipawin Journal and several other publications, offered me a position as ad sales representative. Otto, a decent Christian man, cut me plenty of slack during the early learning period. In a while, I got a handle on things and sales revenues began to climb.

In any kind of sales, it is essential to establish a good working relationship with clients and potential customers. I seemed to be well accepted in the community, for the most part. A few business people however, seemed strangely unfriendly, even unaccountably hostile toward me. I was puzzled by this and wondered if it was a holdover from some mismanagement in the papers history, or whether it was that Otto was a bold Christian, and now it was known that I was one, too. Whatever the reasons, there were six instances of this kind of animosity over a four month period. Strangely, each time I was mistreated in some way, it seemed the Lord retaliated with a blow that was both swift and damaging.

It started one morning as I called on a TV and electronics store that I had never visited before. When I entered, the proprietor, a heavy-set, middle-aged man rose from a chair at the far side of the room. I introduced myself as representing the local paper; that's about as far as I got. His visage, already dour, became most unfriendly, and he loosed a tirade denouncing the paper and everyone connected with it. He said, "I wouldn't advertise my products in that miserable rag even if it didn't cost me a cent! Besides, if I ever get stupid enough to want anything to do with the Journal, I got a phone! I can call! So what are you doin' here?"

"Hmm...Well..." I stammered, "I'm sorry you feel that way, but I guess we know where we stand."

"Damn right," he snorted, then turned his back and went back to his chair.

I left.

That Saturday night a half-ton jumped the curb and plowed through the show-window of that electronics store. Half the inventory was wiped out, and the building was in shambles. The business never reopened.

A couple of weeks later I called the owner of a small restaurant and lunch counter on the north side of town. I made an appointment to meet the woman at the restaurant at ten the next morning.

I arrived on time the next day, made myself acquainted with a waitress and asked her to notify the owner that I was there. The girl conferred with her employer upstairs then told me that her boss was busy and would not see me.

I gave the young waitress my business card and asked her to remind her employer that we had a 10 o-clock appointment.

The girl returned, quite embarrassed, "Charlene says she doesn't want to see you, she won't be advertising in your paper, and you should stop bothering her," she related.

I was annoyed. "You tell Charlene she doesn't have to worry," I said, "I won't be back."

That night, a car leaped the curb and nearly demolished the entire lunchroom! The building, which was quite old, was ultimately torn down.

I sold an ad campaign to the owner of a hair salon on Main Street. We ran his ads for several weeks, and then he called Otto very late one night, claiming I had lied to him and misrepresented the details of the campaign, plus many other things that were not true.

Otto chastised him for not discussing it with me, and told him never to call him at home again.

Otto was still a little steamed about it the next morning. I don't know how you want to handle this," he said, "but whatever you want to do, we'll do."

"I want to pull his ads," I replied, "and I want a check, refunding everything he's paid thus far."

"I don't like the word, refund," Otto responded, "but we'll do it." The check was on my desk in minutes.

I went to the salon and confronted Jack. "I'm here for three reasons, Jack." I announced. "First, here's a check refunding everything you've paid. Second, your ads are pulled. Third, I am disappointed that you wouldn't talk to me about your concerns, but called Otto, and even told him things that were not true. I'd like an explanation."

Since Jack had no sensible explanation and did not want to talk to me, I soon left. On my way back to the office, I saw a man running toward me. As he drew nearer I recognized Brian from the Journal, he was carrying his camera. "Where ya going in such a hurry, Brian?" I shouted.

"The hair salon," he puffed, "Just got a call that a car went through the front window!"

I fell into step and we loped the two blocks back to Jack's salon.

All too astonishingly, true! A car rested almost entirely inside the front window. Only one hind wheel remained outside. It was slowly rotating. There was glass everywhere. Two chairs were smashed, and display counters and products were shattered and strewn about. I thanked God that because it was so early in the morning there were no customers in those chairs, and that no one was slashed by flying glass.

Apparently, the driver, angle parking out front had accidentally hit the accelerator instead of the brake.

Jack was finished as a salon owner; however, the building was repaired to house another business.

By this time, I was feeling a little uneasy about these three occurrences. It seemed more than coincidental yet there was nothing conclusive. I was very busy and soon put it out of my mind.

A short time later, I made a sales pitch to the proprietor of a small grocery store. The man was arrogant, in fact downright snotty. He tried to humiliate me in front of some customers in his store.

Rejection is a common experience that sales people come to know well. Every day customers decline, even after a fine presentation. However, abuse and humiliation are uncalled for. A simple, 'no' we can all handle.

I prayed a lot about my demeanor as a salesman. I asked the Lord for a gracious spirit to handle rejection and the occasional instance of mistreatment. I was able to stay clear of anger or bitterness, because of the Lord's help.

Before the week was over the arrogant grocer's store took fire at night, and burned to the ground. Not a thing was saved.

In the meantime, I had submitted a proposal to the owner of a large meat shop and abattoir on the south side. When I called to discuss it, the man informed me in clear terms of his contempt for the Journal, its circulation, its news coverage and its staff. He practically invited me to leave the premises.

This kind of thing I found hard to take. First, the Journal was an excellent paper. Otto and his staff were skilful and hard working. Furthermore, not a business in town was operated with more honesty and integrity.

I put it into the Lord's hands and asked Him to forgive the butcher's ignorance and to help me do the same.

Several weeks later Otto was traveling out of town to Star City, where the company's web press was located. As he approached the south side, he spotted smoke. It was the abattoir and meat shop. While Otto immediately phoned the Fire Department, the flames raced through the frame buildings and in minutes, they were an inferno. There was nothing he could do…except to get out his trusty camera and record the dramatic demise of a business, frame-by-frame.

It seems appropriate that a four-column photo of one spectacular fire graced the front page of the next issue of the Nipawin Journal! The picture was enhanced by a superbly written eyewitness account.

By now there seemed to be a pattern emerging that caused me deep concern. I prayed about it several times but found no satisfaction.

I traveled to a nearby city, representing a new, mass-distribution publication that Otto had recently founded. I called on a large, three-story department store, hoping to convince them to spend some advertising dollars in our new publication. I located the management offices on the second floor. A receptionist went to the General Manager's office and informed him that I was there.

As I watched George Brand stride purposefully toward me, I observed that he was a stocky man, perhaps in his early forties. He had short, dark hair and a swarthy complexion, and he wore a scowl that looked like it fit him all too well. He did not invite me to his office, choosing rather to deal with me in the reception area, in front of the office staff.

I introduced myself and handed him my business card.

He glanced at it and shoved it back at me, then launched into the most disgusting stream of invective I had ever encountered in my fledgling career in advertising. He was ignorant, he was profane, he was abusive, and he attacked me, personally. The words just poured out!

I was taken aback and speechless, not that I had a chance to respond anyway.

At last, he seemed to have said his piece. He turned away, and then whirled around for a final shot. "And don't bother coming back!" he snarled, "If there's going to be any contact with your publication, I'll do the calling." With that, he stomped into his office and closed the door.

It was humiliating. It was embarrassing. And it was public. Old stirrings from the life before I became a Christian began to stealthily surface. I boxed for years as a young man; in those days, I settled such issues swiftly. I asked the Lord's help to remain calm.

Several of the office staff gathered around. "Don't take it personally," one said, "that man is an imbecile. He doesn't know how to treat people."

"He's an ass!" the receptionist said.

"I can't argue with that," I responded. "Anyway thanks for your encouragement. I guess I won't be back."

Well, I did come back! I came back the following week, and my first stop in the city was that Department Store. During the week, that building was gutted by fire! The destruction was unbelievable. The whole structure was reduced to a giant mound of blackened rubble that looked like photos of bombed-out buildings in World War II.

Now I saw the full picture; and the knowledge of it staggered me. In those few months, people representing six businesses had mistreated me. Every one of those businesses was destroyed! Was this the Lord's doing? Was He doing this on my behalf? I had to believe it was so, and yet it was too awesome to consider; my mind could not process it.

I found a verse of Scripture that sheds some light on these things. Isaiah 41:11 *"Behold all those who were incensed against you shall be ashamed and disgraced; they shall be as nothing, and those who strive with you shall perish."* It was His care over Israel those centuries ago. We need to remember that He loves us, too, with an everlasting love. Romans 12:19 reads- *"Beloved, do not avenge your-selves, but rather give place to wrath; for it is written, "Vengeance is Mine, I will repay,' says the Lord."*

We believe that primarily, God's vengeance is ex-acted at the final judgment. However, I believe I received a frightening glimpse of it being meted out in this life.

CHAPTER 23

YOU GOTTA START SOMEWHERE

Reverend Gary Ziehl was a bon-a-fide evangelist. The Holy Spirit anointed him to win souls, and he was very proficient at his craft.

I first met Gary when we both lived in Nipawin, Saskatchewan. Later, when I responded to the call into full-time ministry, I invited the evangelist to conduct special meetings at various churches I pastored.

One fall, I arranged with Ziehl to minister for a week at my church in eastern Saskatchewan. The congregation prayed faithfully, we advertised the meetings well, and on the first night, the sanctuary was packed. Gary preached a powerful salvation message and extended an appeal to any who wished to receive Christ. It was as though those in the pews were from another planet. No one responded. No one responded on the second night, either.

At last, on the third evening, an elderly woman seated near the back, lifted a hand. The evangelist and I spoke with her after the service. She was a gray-haired Ukrainian widow in her mid-sixties. She said her name was Nina, and that she attended a large, formal church on the north side. "But they don't preach things like this," she said.

Nina was a very forthright and 'up-front' sort of person; and there was no uncertainty in her choice to humble herself and receive Christ as her Savior. I could see that the experience was very real to her.

The next day, as Ziehl and I discussed the meetings, I wondered about the fact that so far only one person had responded.

Gary was not concerned. "You gotta start somewhere," he said. "Perhaps this little lady will be the key God uses to open the way for many others. He was right. Each evening for the rest of the week, other folks received Christ as Savior, too.

That fourth night Nina brought her daughter, her son-in-law and their two children, a boy of nine and his sister, twelve. All four of them gave their hearts to Jesus.

As Gary and I talked with the family, Nina mentioned that Alex, her grandson, had a congenital heart defect and could do nothing strenuous, especially sports.

I asserted that the same Jesus, who has power to forgive and to save, also has power to heal, today. Soon the evangelist and I laid hands on the young boy in Jesus' name, and the Lord mercifully and miraculously healed him, on the spot! What jubilation there was in that little family, especially in Alex!

In talking with the boy several weeks later, I said, "Jesus has done a wonderful thing for you, Alex."

"Oh Yes!" Alex exclaimed, "Every day I kneel down by my bed and I thank Jesus for what He did for me. Now I'm just like other boys, I can even play hockey."

The meetings continued for the week and we rejoiced greatly, because a number of people had given their hearts to the Lord Jesus in that time. It all began with one little gray-haired woman, but it did not end there. Moreover, it did not end when the special meetings ended, either.

Nina, her family and some others began to attend our regular services. One evening in the mid-week service, Nina stood up. "Pastor," she said, "I have stomach ulcers. I have been receiving medical attention for quite a while, but it helps very little. It is very troublesome and painful, and there are so many things that I cannot eat. Do you think Jesus would heal me?"

"Why don't we ask Him?" I replied, "We'll pray right now." We gathered around Nina and prayed earnestly for her healing.

Early the next morning Nina phoned me at home. "Pastor," she almost shouted over the phone, "I went home from prayer-meeting last night and I had a meal like I haven't had in years. I fried a steak with onions; I had sauerkraut and dill pickles, everything I have not been able to eat for so long. Then I went to bed and slept like a baby all night! Praise the Lord, Pastor Lee, I've been healed!"

A few weeks later, again at the mid-week service, Nina was a little downcast. "It's my two year old granddaughter in Regina," she explained, she's in the Pasqua Hospital with eczema over most of her body. It is so painful and nothing they are doing is helping. Pastor could you go to Regina and pray for her?"

"I certainly could," I replied, but somehow, I don't think I need to. We're going to pray for your granddaughter by proxy, right now. We'll lay our hands on you, in her place."

"Can Jesus heal people at a distance like that?" she enquired.

"Absolutely," I assured her, "He can do anything!"

The faithful flock gathered around Nina once again, and prayed, this time for her granddaughter miles away in Regina.

On Sunday morning, Nina was on her feet quickly to testify about another miracle. "Jesus has done it!" she exclaimed through tears, "Overnight the baby's skin became totally clear. The doctors don't know how it happened, but we do! How wonderful Jesus is!" she cried.

A week before Christmas Nina's daughter, Arlene called to inform me that Lisa, her daughter was in the hospital. The doctors had diagnosed rheumatic fever, and were considering sending her to Regina.

Lisa was twelve, a very pretty young girl. Neverthe-less, as I looked at her in that hospital bed I knew she was also a very sick young girl. Her face was flushed and she had a very high fever.

"Oh Pastor," she sighed, "I don't feel well at all, and they tell me I likely won't be able to go home for Christmas. They might even send me to Regina." Her eyes welled with tears.

Something stirred deep inside of me, almost like a holy anger. "You know, Lisa," I said, "we haven't talked to Jesus about this yet. You just might be going home for Christmas after all."

"Oh Pastor Lee," the girl cried hopefully, "could Jesus heal me? Would He heal me?"

"He loves you, Lisa," I responded, "and nothing is too hard for Him."

I opened the Bible to Luke 4:38, 39, and read of the day Peter's mother in law was in bed with a high fever. Jesus rebuked the fever, it left, and the woman was healed. "I'm going to stand in the place of Jesus, today," I explained, "and I'm going to rebuke this fever just like Jesus did."

"I know Jesus healed my brother, Alex," she said, "and He healed my Grandma. I believe he will heal me, too!"

I stood over her and rebuked the fever as though it had a conscious intelligence. I commanded it to leave Lisa's body, in Jesus' name. Then I laid a hand on her forehead and asked the Lord to flow through her by His healing Spirit and make her completely well.

Immediately the girl sat up. "I feel better," she announced. "In fact, I feel good! My head is not hurting like it was, my body is not aching and I don't feel hot anymore!"

She certainly looked well, and her face was no longer flushed.

"Feel my face," she said, "Feel my face, its cool!"

I touched her cheek with the back of my hand. "You're as cool as a cucumber!" I exclaimed.

I called a nurse into the room. "Will you take this girl's temperature?" I asked.

"Don't need to," she retorted, "I checked her half an hour ago."

"Feel her face," I suggested.

The nurse touched Lisa's face, and immediately reached for a thermometer. I could see she noticed the clear eyes and normal color, too. When she withdrew the thermometer and checked it's reading, I said, "Well?"

"Her temperature is normal!" the nurse announced in astonishment.

"Jesus healed me," Lisa explained calmly.

The nurse glanced at me, then at Lisa. "Wow!" she said quietly, and scurried out of the room.

During the time I had been ministering to Lisa, a boy of about ten, limped into the room, climbed up on the foot of the bed and observed everything silently. I had ignored him.

Now I turned to the boy. "Hi," I said, "I'm Pastor Lee. What's your name?"

"I'm Tom," the boy said, "I'm in the next room."

"Why do they have you in here, Tom?" I queried.

"It's my hip," he explained, "it hurts all the time. I can hardly walk anymore. I've been in here a week and they can't find out what is wrong. Now they're sending me to Regina."

"Do you know about Jesus?" I asked.

"Oh yes!" Tom returned, "I have Jesus in my heart. I go to Sunday School at the Lutheran Church."

"That's wonderful, Tom!" I replied. "Do you think Jesus could heal your hip, today?"

"I do now!" he answered, "He just healed Lisa, didn't He?"

I turned to the girl. "Well, Lisa," I asked, "Do you think Jesus would like to heal Tom?"

"I know He would!" she responded quickly.

"Let's lay our hands on Tom, together," I suggested. "You know, I believe Jesus can hardly wait to heal this boy." We laid our hands on Tom, and I prayed a simple prayer. The presence of Jesus was very strong in that room.

"Sometimes when Jesus was helping people He told them to rise up and walk," I explained, "So, Tom, in Jesus' name, rise up and walk!"

Without a word, the boy slid to the edge of the bed, dangled his feet and carefully reached for the floor. He stood and took a couple of careful steps. "It don't hurt," he said. He took several more bold strides. "It don't hurt at all!" he shouted. With that, Tom ran out of the room and down the broad hall. I heard him shout, "I'm healed! Jesus has healed me!"

Those two kids went home for Christmas, and they went home completely well! They also went home with a new and a precious understanding of the love of God, and of the compassion and of the power of Jesus. I did too.

Many people have experienced the touch of God on their lives since that little, gray-haired grandmother gave her heart to Jesus in the evangelistic meeting. It would be humanly impossible to trace the path of the Holy Spirit through that family and far beyond, to the present day. As Gary Ziehl said, "You've gotta start somewhere." Only God knows what the final result will be.

CHAPTER 24

CHILD-LIKE FAITH

My youngest son, Dan, was an energetic and determined little fellow, as a child. He also possessed an amazing sensitivity to spiritual things at a very early age. His exuberance got him into trouble from time to time, but his spiritual bent taught me some things about faith, more than once.

Once, when Danny was about two, he was playing a game of hide-and-seek, with his older sister, Janet. He hid behind the bedroom door. Janet pretended she did not know where he was hiding so he stuck his fingers through the crack in the door, adjacent to the hinges. The door began to swing shut, trapping his fingers. At his cry, Janet rushed to the door and inadvertently pulled it the wrong way. The extreme leverage crushed Danny's tiny fingers.

The boy screamed in pain and began to cry out, "Daddy pray to Jesus! Daddy pray to Jesus!"

My heart sank as I looked at those little fingers, already completely black, and with an angry red line through the second finger. I sat on the bed and sat Danny on my lap, facing away from me. I held the injured hand between my two hands. I confess that my faith seemed at low ebb, but I was overwhelmed with a fierce compassion for my hurting little son. I cried out desperately to the Lord for mercy. In a short time, the presence of Jesus became so strong it seemed as though we were enveloped in an invisible cloud of His love and power. Soon, I noticed that Danny had not only stopped screaming but he was not crying at all. I sneaked a sidelong peek; he seemed unconcerned and was looking around the room.

I ended my prayer and we sat silently for a minute or two. Then, very slowly, I opened my hands. He withdrew his small hand and held it up before us. There was not a mark on it!

He slowly rotated his hand several times and examined it closely, working his fingers freely. He then turned, and looking up into my face, he held his now perfectly whole hand before me and asked solemnly, "Where da marks go?"

"Jesus took the marks away," I replied.

He began to laugh and clap his hands. He jumped off my knee and skipped through the house clapping and shouting, "Jesus took da marks away! Jesus took da marks away!"

I closed the bedroom door and spent a while praising and thanking the Christ who could show such mercy and compassion to a little one in his pain, despite the fumbling faith of a distraught father.

Late one afternoon I came home early from work. I noticed little Danny kneeling at the front steps of the house. He was bowed down and motionless. I guessed he was watching the cat under the steps. I tiptoed closer, thinking I would surprise him. As I drew near, I was astonished to hear, he was praying. Even more surprisingly, he was praying meaningful prayers! Then, he raised small hands heavenward and began to praise and worship God. This was not child's play; the boy was communicating with God.

I felt embarrassed to be eavesdropping on such a holy thing. I tiptoed away and entered the house by the side door.

Later, in the house, I picked him up and asked, "Do you pray to Jesus, sometimes?"

"Oh yes!" he replied, eyes sparkling, "Jesus loves me."

"You bet He does!" I assured him. "Oh Lord," I prayed silently in my heart, "what a gracious thing You are doing in this special child. May he never, ever lose this reality."

We were living in the northern Saskatchewan village of White Fox, in those days. Our house was located on a corner lot in a nice area of town. One Saturday afternoon I was trimming the hedge and Danny was playing nearby. As he ran up the flagstone walk, he tripped and fell, skinning both knees quite badly. Blood ran freely from lacerations on both bare knees. "Daddy pray to Jesus, Daddy pray to Jesus," he sobbed.

I sat down on the wishing well in the front yard and lifted him onto my lap. It was Saturday afternoon, and this was a busy corner lot; I decided to pray with dignity. I covered my face with my hands and mumbled my requests quietly.

After a few minutes of this, I was interrupted; Danny pulled my hands away from my face and looking up tearfully he wailed, "Dad, don't pray like that, I'm really hurting!"

I was stunned. What a rebuke! Here was my young son needing a healing touch from the Lord, and looking to me to bring the help of God into his need. However, I was too full of pride to pray openly and whole-heartedly. I felt so ashamed! I asked forgiveness of the Lord and then began to pray in earnest. I cried! I shouted! I spoke in tongues!

In a few minutes, I was interrupted again. The same small voice said, cheerfully, "I'm okay now Dad, Jesus heard you this time!"

By this time, there was no turning back, I praised and thanked the Lord fully and fervently. I think the passers by hustled on a little faster than usual, probably wondering what those crazy Christians were up to. If they only knew...

When Danny was seven, we lived in a small, eastern Saskatchewan town. I was the pastor of the local Pentecostal church.

One Sunday evening I felt especially drawn to encourage the congregation to receive the fullness of the Holy Spirit in a new and a greater measure. I realized that some of the folks had had little teaching about the baptism of the Holy Spirit and others were skeptical about the matter of speaking in other tongues as described in the Book of Acts. I reminded them about the necessity of not only being filled with the Spirit, but also walking under the Spirit's direction and His power. I taught them afresh of the desirability of being able to pray, and praise and worship the Lord in that supernatural language of prayer called speaking in other tongues.

At the conclusion of the sermon, my wife, Beverly, knew it was time to take Danny home and get him to bed. He had listened carefully at times, but finally had become fidgety; no doubt, he was bored with the duration of the adult service.

"C'mon Danny," Bev said, "lets go home to bed."

"No Mom," the boy replied, "I can't go home now, Jesus wants to fill me with the Spirit, just like Dad said."

Something about the earnestness of his countenance caused my wife to reconsider. "All right," she conceded, "but I want you to go and sit in the front pew."

I was a little surprised to see the seven-year-old take a seat at the front. His feet didn't reach the floor; he swung them back and forth, alternately. He leaned forward, though, and was very attentive.

I took up the guitar and began to lead the people in some worship songs. "When your heart is open to give the Lord true praise and worship," I admonished, "it is also open to Him. Jesus can fill an open heart with His Spirit and His blessings. Let us open our hearts and worship Him."

The people responded freely, but there was one voice that cut through all the adult sounds; it was the small, pure voice of the one on the front pew singing to the Jesus he knew.

I was deeply moved, so were many others.

Then, the boy paused and raised both hands in an act of worship. His small frame began to tremble as the precious Holy Spirit settled upon him. Once again, the small voice rang out clearly, this time speaking words of praise and worship in a language he had never learned.

It was as though somewhere a great switch turned on; suddenly, the Holy Spirit swept over us all! We were all filled with the Holy Spirit, and we all spoke with other tongues as the Spirit gave us utterance, just as on the Day of Pentecost.

I have never participated in a meeting quite like that one; where the Spirit of God revealed Himself in such a wonderful way, and where no one was left untouched. Some who had grown cold or discouraged in their Christian experience were revived and refilled with the Spirit. Some who had never experienced the Spirit's power in their lives were baptized in the Holy Spirit, and joined everyone else in praising God in other tongues. One board member who was 42 years of age confided that he had received the baptism in the Holy Spirit at camp when he was 14. "I've never sensed the power of the Spirit like this, or spoken in tongues again, until tonight," he said tearfully.

Another said his spiritual life had been dry and difficult for years, but in that meeting; something happened, the heaviness left, his joy and the reality of Jesus returned.

Many others testified of great blessings. The truth is that an entire congregation was raised to a new level of spiritual life, and the key that opened the door to that outpouring of the grace of God was the child-like faith of a seven-year-old boy.

CHAPTER 25

THE PRESENCE OF GOD

We have heard a lot about the 'presence of God.' Undoubtedly, this phrase has different meanings to different people. As an older brother who has had the holy privilege of witnessing the Lord demonstrate His power for some years, I have come to the conclusion that, for me at least, the 'presence of the Lord,' is when the Holy Spirit makes real to our spiritual senses that Jesus is alive from the dead and He is present with us, now. The Spirit imparts an inner certainty that Christ dwells in us, He is with us, in our presence; and we are with Him, in His presence. Some have called it the 'felt presence of God.'

Jesus, Himself said, *"I will never leave you nor forsake you."* It takes the power of the Holy Spirit, however, to reveal the truth of this word to us in actual experience. When the Holy Spirit is revealing the presence of Jesus, prayer is easy, faith rises to a new level, and the power of God is often demonstrated in a remarkable way.

I witnessed this one Sunday evening in our small prairie church. I had invited an Indian singing group for a gospel music concert. They sang well and testified powerfully of the grace of God in their lives. One dark-skinned woman was mightily anointed as she related to us a story of the mercy and the power of Jesus who had set her free from the bondage of sin. When she sang, the sense of the presence of the Lord was so strong that the hairs on the back of my neck stood up. That awesome presence touched us all.

At the conclusion of the concert I asked the congregation to rise and sing, "I am Thine O Lord," the wonderful old hymn written by Fanny Crosby. Those great words penned so long ago, truly expressed the sentiments of most of us that night.

After the dismissal, Percy, an elderly man who lived across the street from the church, sought me out. "Pastor," he exclaimed, "this has been a wonderful evening! I have never sensed the presence of the Lord so powerfully before. Something happened to me when I began to sing the first line of that hymn, 'I am Thine O Lord,' It's as though my eyes were opened, and somehow I knew it's true! I am His, He is mine, He is alive, He loves me, and He is here! For some reason I took a deep breath, and Pastor, I breathed all the way down for the first time in years!"

I did not know what Percy meant so he explained, "I've had emphysema for years and I haven't been able to take a full, deep breath for a long time. But I was healed singing the first line of that hymn! Praise the Lord, He is wonderful and He is here!"

It was true; Percy's lungs were miraculously restored. Nobody had prayed for him. Nobody anointed him with oil. Nobody laid hands on him. When the Holy Spirit makes us know that Jesus is present, anything can happen!

I observed that same phenomenon late the same year in that little church. Our mid-week prayer service was a highlight for those who were the most serious about spiritual things. Often 30 or more attended. Most times, I would lead a time of praise and worship with the guitar, and then have a Bible study followed by a meaningful prayer time.

One evening I felt strangely burdened in my soul. Somehow, it just did not seem appropriate to sing at the time, so I slipped quietly into the front pew. I just sat silently and prayed. The usual crowd was present. Some quietly chatted, while they waited for the service to commence. Soon they all fell silent and I sensed that they too were quietly in prayer.

We must have sat quietly for about fifteen minutes. It was a silent but spiritually powerful time. We were sensing the presence of Jesus.

Suddenly, as though an invisible conductor had stepped to the podium, tapped his baton and indicated the downbeat, all of us at the same moment, burst forth singing in other tongues as the Spirit gave us utterance! It was supernatural, and it was as marvelous as it was powerful!

I have been in many services where worshippers sang in the Spirit, sometimes thousands of them. Often it has been a beautiful and a moving experience. However, this time of spiritual worship was much different than any I had previously experienced. The harmony was flawless, the cadence impeccable. Our voices rose in thunderous crescendos and gave way to soft pianissimos. Melody and volume rose and fell under the precise and masterful direction of the Holy Spirit, Himself. It is hard to describe the sense of joy, and awe and reality.

I do not really know how long this went on, perhaps ten or fifteen minutes. Our singing gradually slowed and softened, then, as though there had been one final stroke of the baton, 'finis,' every voice ceased at the same instant! It was as though the conductor had laid his baton on the podium, bowed to the right, bowed to the left, and left the platform…it was over.

Every one of us sat in silence again. The thought came, that I am the pastor, I should rise up and say something, or do something, or explain something. Thankfully, I dismissed the notion.

Then, from the left, at the back came a prophecy, distinct, strong, and insightful, then another across the aisle. Someone began to praise the Lord, then a chorus of praise swept across the sanctuary. Soon we were worshipping Him in Spirit and in truth.

After a while, the praise subsided, and someone began to pray, deep, Spirit-prompted groanings of intercession. A season of mighty prayer followed, until once again we sat in silence. No one felt that they were required to do something, or take leadership. This is called, waiting on God.

At length, we were jolted by a new direction the meeting seemed to be taking. One of the board members, who was manager of the local lumberyard, began to shout, "Pastor, some of you guys, come over here!"

I went over with some of the men to where Larry sat in the front pew. I was surprised and a little concerned to see him unbuckle his belt, zip down, and begin to pull down his underwear.

"Whoa! Whoa! Hold on!" I cautioned.

"Look! Look!" He jabbered.

"I don't see nothing but your bare belly," Big Jim growled.

"That's it exactly!" Larry exclaimed, "there's nothing! You see I injured myself lifting planks at the yard. I have a hernia and I have been wearing a truss for two years. Look, it's completely gone! I've been healed just sitting here in the presence of God!"

No one prayed for Larry. He didn't even think about his need, nor did he ask for healing that night, but when the Spirit of God gets to reveal the Son of God to the people of God, anything can happen!

Truly, this young man had received a notable miracle, but none of us considered that the highlight of the night. All of us had been touched to the very core of our being by the ministry of the precious Holy Spirit.

I doubt if any one was more deeply moved than I was. I got to do absolutely no act of leadership that whole evening, thank God. It was all Him! The closest I came to assuming a pastoral role was a final prayer of benediction. Then we all filed out, each one quietly thanking God for such a unique and holy experience.

CHAPTER 26

BIG ANSWER TO A SMALL PRAYER

Pastoring a small church in western Canada has its advantages and its disadvantages. The downside is that because of small congregations, finances can be tight. The upside is that the whole congregation can become like a large family, with friendly and informal relationships. Ideally, the pastor just relaxes and becomes a member of this caring group.

I was the pastor of such a church in the 1970s. They taught me a lot, and it seemed like we all pretended that I was the spiritual one.

One day I received a call that Trudy, one of our members, had had a bad fall and injured herself, considerably. I went to the hospital and was informed that she had been taped up, sent home, and that bed rest had been prescribed for at least a week.

I drove across town to her modest bungalow and knocked on the door. Hearing no answer, I tried the door, found it unlocked and shouted inside, "Anybody home?"

Just about to leave, I heard a feeble voice inviting me in. I stepped inside and called out again. Trudy answered from the bedroom, "Have a seat, Pastor, I'll come out and make tea."

"No, no!" I replied, "I'll make the tea, you just rest."

"Certainly not!" she snapped rather curtly, "I'll serve the tea, you just have a seat."

"Okay, okay," I responded, and sat down on a chair in the kitchen.

Trudy seemed to be taking a long time to appear. I soon discovered why; she shuffled out of the bedroom, sidewise, supporting herself hand-over-hand against the wall. Her progress was painful and slow as she was only able to manage about six inch steps with her shuffling, sidewise gait.

Very concerned, I jumped up and admonished her to sit down and permit me to make the tea. She objected adamantly, informing me that she was the host in her own house and would indeed be serving. She painfully negotiated her way around the kitchen, and, at a snails pace, brewed a pot of tea, set out cups and produced a generous plate of cookies from a colorful jar on the shelf. All of this must have taken nearly half an hour and was painful to watch. As she worked however, we were able to chat and she told me how she sustained her injury.

Trudy was an energetic German woman in her early forties. At the time, she was caring for a foster child, a rambunctious young boy of eight or nine. The lad was quite mischievous and unaccustomed to discipline. Trudy was attempting to address this behavioral shortcoming in a kindly but firm manner. Apparently, the boy had taken something, and when Trudy insisted he put it back, he refused, saying she would have to catch him, first. The youngster skipped nimbly across the living room, the woman, half in fun, pursued. The young fellow leaped over the coffee table, Trudy tripped on the rug and fell across the table, cracking several ribs as well as inflicting some cartilage damage.

With tea finally ready, my host eased herself into a chair and poured it. "Pastor," she asked, "will you ask the blessing?"

"Certainly," I replied, and began to give thanks for the lunch. It came to my mind that I should pray for Trudy in her distress, and ask the Lord to bring about a speedy recovery. As I prayed, I reached over and laid a hand on her shoulder.

She began to fidget, and I could feel her moving about vigorously. I chanced a peek; she was reaching around with her right hand, grabbing at the injured area of her left side. Suddenly she screamed and leaped straight up! The chair crashed over backwards, and my German parishioner bounded into the living room shouting at the top of her voice! I could not make out what she was saying, perhaps some of it was German, but mostly it sounded like unintelligible yelling. She traversed the living room in robust strides. I noticed she cleared the coffee table with plenty to spare!

The house featured a lengthy island, which the dining area, living room, hall and kitchen encircled. Dumbfounded, I watched the excited woman begin her second circuit around the island. Finally, it dawned on me that Trudy was not entirely berserk, but was praising God in some kind of unbridled, super-demonstrative fashion.

I remained in my chair throughout the whole episode. As she completed her second revolution around the island, I was now more curious than alarmed. She stopped at the table, breathless, but beaming. "Pastor," she shouted, "I am completely healed! I have absolutely no pain! Look!" she exclaimed, pounding her fist against the injured area of her left rib cage. "I tell you I am totally whole!"

I righted her overturned chair. "Sit down, Trudy," I said, "and tell me about it."

Trudy sat down, still breathing hard and quite excited. "When you prayed, I felt the power of God go through me," she said. "I could feel gentle hands touching my ribs, healing the injuries and relieving the pain. I reached around but there was nothing there. Then I realized it was Jesus…What a joy just to know, He knows and He cares! I guess I was out of control a little bit, wasn't I."

"Yeah, you were a little nuts alright," I agreed, "but I can't think of a better reason."

CHAPTER 27

JESUS, JUST IN TIME

As a pastor, I usually visited the hospital each week. In small towns, local protocol is refreshingly informal. There is no rule that pastors can only call on patients from their own denomination. My practice was to pray a lot and ask the Lord to direct me by His Spirit to those I should be sure to visit, regardless of their church affiliation; the other pastors did the same.

One afternoon as I walked down the hospital corridor I glanced in a room and saw a man sitting on a bed with his back toward me. It seemed the Spirit impressed me to enter that room. I stepped in and paused, the man was tense and hunched over, and I could see he was in great pain. He was oblivious to my presence; I just waited and prayed.

After a time, he relaxed a little as though the pain had eased somewhat, then he noticed me. I carefully sat down beside him and said, "I see you're having a lot of pain."

He nodded, "Cancer," he said. "I've had it for a while but the last couple of months the pain has been unbearable."

I judged he was a man in his late sixties, graying and baldish, not a large man.

He noticed I carried a Bible. "Are you a minister?" he asked.

I nodded. "Pentecostal," I replied. "Do you have a church affiliation?"

"No," the man replied quickly, "I've never gone to church; I don't know anything about God or the Bible at all."

"It's very important for every one of us to come to terms with God," I said gently, "You know we'll all stand before Him one day."

"I know," the small man said earnestly. "I believe there is a God, but I don't know how to reach Him. I don't know what He requires of me, and I am very frightened about what will happen to me. There is nothing more they can do about this cancer; they say I am going to die soon. Can you help me?"

My heart went out to him in compassion. He looked like a decent man, a kindly man, but his face was deeply etched by pain and fear.

"God has a way of sending us help when we need it most," I said. "And I believe He sent me here because He sees that you need His help today." I opened the Bible and began to share the Bread of Life with a hurting and dying man. He seemed starved to hear about Jesus. Several times he urged, "Read more, tell me more."

At last, he sat back and with tears in his eyes he said, "Jesus is so wonderful! From what you have said, it seems He could even love a man like me. Maybe there is a place in heaven for me. I want to give my heart to Jesus, if He will have me. Will you help me do it?"

We bowed there, I helped him pray and, in a moment, the greatest Gift that God has for man became his possession. The man's countenance was transformed before my eyes! The deep lines of his face were softened. The lifeless, pain-filled eyes had a new sparkle. He smiled, even laughed. "I've never felt like this before in my whole life! I have such a peace, right here!" he exclaimed, putting a hand on the center of his chest. "And Reverend, for the first time in months I have absolutely no pain in my body! Thank You Jesus!" he cried. "This is so wonderful; Jesus is everything you said, and more! I have no pain. I don't feel sick, and I'm not afraid anymore because Jesus is with me and He loves me." The words flowed freely from his mouth.

Then the rejoicing little man became somber for a moment. "You know, Reverend Lee, I've never felt this good, but I'm so tired," he said. "Because of the pain and the fear, I've never really slept for months, but now I have such peace, I know I can. Would it be all right if I just had a sleep right now? Jesus won't leave me will He?"

"He will never leave you!" I assured him. "And yes, get some sleep."

The man stretched out on the bed and I pulled the covers over him. His face radiated a gentle peace.

"Reverend, I want you to promise you'll come back soon and read the Bible and tell me more about Jesus." His voice was almost pleading.

"I promise," I replied. "It's nearly two o-clock now, at two tomorrow I'll be here and we'll read, and talk and pray some more."

"Oh thank you," he responded, "please don't forget."

"Not a chance! I'll be here," I said. I prayed a brief prayer and tiptoed out, because he was asleep before I got to the amen.

At two the next afternoon I strode quickly to room seventeen, eager to fellowship with God's new child. The room was empty. All three beds were made up neatly, but they were unoccupied. I hustled back to the main desk and asked the nurse where they had moved the man from room seventeen.

The nurse looked at me strangely, "You don't know?" she queried.

"Know what?" I shot back.

"He passed away yesterday," she replied.

I was dumbfounded, for a moment. "What time yesterday did he pass away?" I finally asked.

She checked some charts, "He died at two," she said.

CHAPTER 28

THE FINANCIAL TEST

The devil has brought failure and discouragement into many lives, through money. Problems can arise if we have too much or too little, or because of coveting it, or employing dishonorable means to acquire it, or even blaming God for the lack of it.

The Lord, too, sometimes uses money as the instrument to test and refine our faith. I observed this being worked out in the life of a godly man one winter, in a small prairie church where I was the pastor. The man's name was Lawrence; he was a deacon, a man in his early fifties. Lawrence shared his money problem in a church board meeting one night. There were six of us present and we quickly understood that our friend was facing a severe challenge regarding money and faith.

This is the story that Lawrence unfolded to us that evening; he said, "I've tried to teach my children about the faithfulness of God. Many times, we have had to trust the Lord for His help. But today my faith is really on the line in a very sensitive area." Deeply moved, he went on, "As you know, my daughter, is in Bible College. I managed to pay for the first semester, now it is nearly time to pay the remainder, and I am broke. If I can't come up with three hundred and fifty, she will have to drop out. What's that going to do to her faith, not to mention mine?" Tears began to trickle down his leathery countenance.

Several of the other men changed position in their chairs; big Jim cleared his throat and prepared to speak.

Lawrence lifted a hand. "No," he said, "I know half of you could write a check to meet this need and you'd never miss it. I know you men," he continued, "I know every one of you would like to help. However, this is not just a money issue; this has become a faith issue. If you men loan me money, that will solve my financial problem, but it will not solve my faith problem. I'm asking you to believe God with me, to help me believe." Lawrence was weeping now. None of us were dry-eyed, either.

"Men," I said, "our brother's faith is being tested over this issue, but ours is, too. Are you ready to put your faith on the line with Lawrence, asking God to meet this need in His own way?"

The men were thoughtful but all agreed. I guess we all needed to see the Lord demonstrate His faithfulness in our midst one more time. Our prayer time that night was powerful and prolonged. We cried out to God in earnest and whole-hearted supplication.

"I feel a peace about this now," Lawrence said later. "I don't know how, but I believe somehow the Lord is going to reveal Himself in this."

Several weeks passed and there was no mention of Lawrence's plight or our prayers. Then, on a Wednesday evening, just before the mid-week prayer service, Lawrence stormed into the church. He was animated and excited, almost jabbering, which was very uncharacteristic of him. "Look Pastor!" he shouted, waving an envelope, "It's the Lord, the Lord has done it Himself!"

"Our prayers have been answered?" I asked.

"Take a look at this!" he almost shouted again. He handed me a sizeable check and an enclosed, penciled letter, obviously written with an unsteady, and not too skilled hand.

"Tell me this story, Lawrence," I said. I had heard him tell of his need, now I wanted to hear him tell of the answer. Eagerly he complied.

It seems that one fall, when Lawrence was in his early twenties, he hired on as a harvest hand with a farmer some distance away. The weather turned wet and the man couldn't pay any of his men what they had earned up to that time. They left. Lawrence stayed. He said, "I won't see you stuck. If you feed me, I will stay and do other work, and when the weather clears, I will help you take off your crop. You pay me when you can."

The man was extremely grateful, but no money changed hands; even though Lawrence did a lot of work for the farmer that fall.

As Lawrence prepared to leave, the farmer thanked him again profusely. He promised that when he got the money, he would pay what he owed, with interest. As he left the yard, Lawrence said that he had absolutely no expectation of ever seeing a dollar from the man, in fact, over time he forgot entirely about the farmer, the farm, and his work.

In that, crudely scrawled letter written thirty years later, the now elderly farmer explained that he had finally sold the farm, got a decent price and moved to town. He had recorded the wage owing Lawrence, calculated interest, and here was the check.

"You know, Pastor," Lawrence confided, "all of this has been a great test of my faith; I didn't handle it very well either. I confess my faith was sagging badly a couple of weeks ago. After we prayed, though, things came into focus again. Now I can't stop praising the Lord!"

"Lawrence," I said, "I want you to tell this story tonight in the service. Show the people the letter. Show the people the check. Let them see, as you have, the reality of the love and the faithfulness of Jesus."

The Lord reached us all that night through His faithful and abundant blessing on one man!

CHAPTER 29

JOHN THE BAPTIST

Our family came to know the Lord through the influence of the First Baptist Church in Aurora, Ontario. We attended that church for the first three years of our spiritual journey. Though I have ministered for many years in a Pentecostal denomination, I nevertheless have a special fondness for the Baptists.

Late one Sunday evening, Percy, a man who lived across the street from the church I was pastoring at the time, informed me that his father-in-law, John, had suffered a massive heart attack. A very concerned Percy asked if I would go to the hospital and pray for John. The prognosis was that the man's condition was hopeless. The doctors expected him to pass away at any time. They had called the family to be at his bedside. Percy and I jumped into my car and were at the hospital in a few minutes.

John's room was directly across from the nurse's station. A heart monitor in the doorway was in full view from inside the room as well the nurse's desk. I shook my head as I viewed the flashing images on the screen. Evidence of a dying man, if I have ever seen it, I thought.

Tears trickled down Percy's cheeks as he looked at the device.

I took a quick breath as we entered the room, it was full of people, sixteen of them. All were family who had quickly gathered. Most stood in small groups, some talking quietly, some weeping.

The head of the bed was set against the center of the east wall. John's wife, Mary, sat at his head on the far side. A nurse sat on the near side. Tubes and wires radiated from the man's body. A light green oxygen mask covered the lower half of John's face. It seemed to accentuate his ghostly pallor. His breathing was irregular and very shallow.

I held out little hope for the man's survival when I entered the room, but, in a moment, the Holy Spirit began to stir me in a deep and powerful way. I heard myself boldly calling for the attention for everyone in the room. "This man needs a miracle!" I said, "And the only One who can help him is the Lord Jesus Christ. Here's what I'm asking you to do," I went on, hardly recognizing the calmness and certainty in my own voice. "If you have absolutely no faith for this, please stand aside and don't participate. If you can believe, even though your faith may be small, come; let's put our faith together. Form a semi-circle around the bed and join hands." Surprisingly, every person complied. They moved into place quickly.

"You, on the far side, take Mary's hand." I instructed. I grasped the hand of the person next to me. The nurse stepped back.

"Now we are a chain of faith," I explained, "Mary and I will lay our hands on John and I will pray, and I believe the power of God is going to flow through us all and touch this man, and heal him!"

By now, the presence of God was mighty in the room, and I felt myself gripped by the Spirit's anointing. In a loud voice, I rebuked the power of death, commanding it in Jesus name, to loose its hold immediately. I then prayed that our hands would be as the hands of Jesus, releasing His healing power to flow through that stricken man and make him completely well.

Instantly, John flinched as though a jolt of high voltage electricity had passed through his body. He thrust his elbows back and heaved into a sitting position. Noticing the oxygen mask, he grabbed it and flung it away. "What's this?" he muttered. His eyes were clear. His face was ruddy and normal. He broke into a grin. "What's going on?" he asked. "What are you people doing here? Where am I, anyway?"

Mary gave a scream of joy, and embraced her husband. People shouted! Everyone talked at once! The nurse rushed back to her position, as though somehow she should be in control, but knew she definitely was not.

I was so overwhelmed at such an amazing demonstration of the mercy, and the power of Jesus, that I could hardly stand. I felt like prostrating myself before Him. I had not been in the room five minutes, yet I knew it was time to leave and let the family rejoice. There was a wonderful joy, and an exhilarating kind of excitement in the room.

As I passed through the door, Percy caught up with me. We stopped to look at the heart monitor. Now the images flashed on its screen in a strong, steady rhythm. "What does that look like to you, Percy?" I queried.

Percy wept. "It looks like the Lord Jesus Christ has been here," he sobbed.

I could not keep the tears back either. "Without a doubt He has," I said.

Before nine the next morning I was at the hospital. The nurse at the desk told me John was in room 14, down the hall. I found him fully dressed and pacing the floor. He looked fit and well, and grabbed me in a bear hug as soon as I stepped into the room.

"Pastor, I'm so glad you've come!" he said, as he stepped over and closed the door.

I started to greet him, but he held up a hand. "Let's praise the Lord for a while, before we talk," he said.

"Well...yeah, sure," I agreed, "I'm with you on that."

Immediately, that Baptist man began to praise and thank the Lord in a very loud voice.

This is not the Baptist way, I thought, remembering the early years of my Christian life. By now, the man was raising his hands and shouting whole-hearted praise. I joined him and together we raised quite a holy ruckus in that hospital room.

After a time we both felt we had adequately expressed our hearts to the Lord, and had a brief but warm-hearted conversation.

"Percy and others told me what went on last night," he began, "I know nothing of it; I didn't even know I was in the hospital. My first recollection is I heard someone speaking the name of Jesus, in a loud voice. Then a great and wonderful power surged through my entire body. Instantly, I was awake," he continued, "and I was well, and I knew it! In fact, I have never felt better in my life than I do at this moment. I have been made perfectly well by the power of God! Furthermore, the doctors can't find a thing wrong with me and I'm getting out of here this morning."

The man who was so marvelously healed that night was a Baptist believer. He and his family attended a little Baptist church about 25 miles north of our town. John was very faithful to his church and his denomination, so much so that some called him, John the Baptist.

The next Sunday, John and his wife showed up at the Pentecostal church for the evening service.

John asked if he could say a few words. "Brothers and sisters," he said, "last Sunday I was dying in the hospital, but the Lord Jesus Christ spared my life and made me perfectly well. I have come here tonight to testify about it, and to praise the Lord with you, for it. I was raised in the Baptist church," he continued, "We were taught that the age of miracles is passed. We did not believe that Jesus heals the sick today as He did two thousand years ago. However, I thank God your pastor believes it! And, I thank God he came and prayed for me, too! I am happy to report that today I am a well man. I have never felt better in my life, thank God, and we came here tonight to praise the Lord with you for everything He has done!"

The old building vibrated with the praises of God's people that night as the congregation rose to give thanks for the wonder of His amazing grace.

CHAPTER 30

FOLLOWING THE FLOW

I was the visiting evangelist in a southern, prairie city one fall weekend. An eager crowd packed the church the first night and the Holy Spirit was revealing Jesus in a special way. After ministering to those who desired to receive Christ as Savior, I asked if there were any who needed to receive healing from the Lord. I was surprised at the number who came forward quickly to fill the entire altar area.

I began to pray for people individually. Then it seemed as though the Lord was drawing me to something different. I had the sense that I was standing in a stream of the love of God that was flowing out into the sanctuary, beyond the seekers at the altar.

I made my way through the crowd and followed the invisible stream to a small, gray-haired woman who was standing by herself, head bowed, weeping. I asked if she needed special prayer. She neither answered nor looked up, she just cried.

The Holy Spirit stirred me deeply and gave a word of knowledge. "You've had back trouble for seven years," I heard myself say. "They have tried to help you in many ways, but at the last visit your doctor said there's nothing more they can do. You have a lot of pain," I said. "The Lord has sent me here to tell you that He loves you. He has seen your tears and heard your prayers, and today you will be healed."

The little woman cried harder, her shoulders shook with her sobs but she neither spoke nor looked up.

I laid my hand on her shoulder and began to speak forcefully. I rebuked her back condition on the authority of Jesus' name. Then I asked Jesus to finish His work and heal her completely.

"Little mother," I said, "the Lord has touched you today. Your back is healed completely and you will never have this trouble again."

The small woman continued to cry. She said not one word and she never raised her head. Through it all, I did not see her face.

Just as strangely and certainly, as I was lead to pray for the woman, I felt released to return and minister to those at the altar.

In a few days, I returned to my pastorate and soon forgot all about the little, gray-haired woman.

Two years later, at a convention of our fellowship in the same city, a small, gray-haired woman with a cheerful countenance approached me. "You're Pastor Updike aren't you?" she asked.

"Yes, I am," I replied. The woman looked familiar.

"I'm the woman with back trouble you prayed for two years ago in the evangelistic meetings," she said. Her face beamed as she went on, "Everything you said that night was absolutely true, and I knew it was Jesus because I hadn't told anyone about the last visit to the doctor. When you prayed, the pain left, and I have been completely well ever since. Look!" she exclaimed, bending down and touching her toes vigorously several times. "I know God loves me, now!" she said with tears of joy.

As I considered her last remark, some things became clearer to me. I was guided by what felt like a stream of love, to minister healing to a person with a great need. While she rejoiced in her healing, the certainty of His love for her is what truly gripped her heart. May God grant us all that certainty, in full measure.

CHAPTER 31

ONE HOUR TO PRAY

Most of the good things that happen in this world happen because somebody prayed. Perhaps the reason we do not pray as much as we should is that we are not aware of just how effective earnest prayer can be. I received an unforgettable reminder about this one fall morning in southern Saskatchewan.

That morning, I received a phone call from a hospital in Regina. Hospital staff informed me that my dad was extremely ill and that his condition was steadily worsening; they suggested I come immediately.

I found out who his doctor was and was able to speak with him. "What's the prognosis?" I asked.

"At best, extremely grave," he replied.

"It sounds as though you don't hold out much hope," I observed.

"Actually no," the doctor responded, "That's why you were called."

"I'm leaving immediately," I said.

Many thoughts flashed through my mind as I headed south and west on that prairie highway. I knew Dad was hospitalized because of a gall bladder ailment, but there was no indication that it was a life threatening matter. Apparently, his health had deteriorated drastically overnight, triggering latent heart problems. I prayed fervently all the way to the city.

I parked and hurried in through the hospitals main doors. I asked the woman at Information about my father. She scanned the register. "He's in ICU," she announced, "but you can't go in there."

"Where's ICU?" I enquired.

"Straight down that hall and to the right," she responded.

"Thanks," I said, and headed down that hall on the double. I hustled quickly into ICU. Obviously, it was a very busy place. The nurse in charge confronted me immediately. "What are you doing in here?" she asked tersely.

"I'm here to see my dad, Ryburn Updike," I replied.

"You can't see your dad and you can't be in here," was the response.

"I can be here," I said firmly, "and I intend to see my dad. First, I am his oldest son. Secondly, I'm a minister of the gospel."

"You'd be in the way and I can't have that," she snapped. "Your dad is dangerously ill and my nurses check his condition every few minutes."

"I'll stay clear," I said. "Every time they come to check on him I'll stand up there by the head of the bed."

"Why do you need to be here, anyway?" she asked.

"This man has got to have a miracle from God," I answered, "and I'm here to pray for him."

The nurse looked me in the eye with a steady gaze. "Okay," she said, yanking open a drawer, "put on this gown and mask and do what you came to do, but if there's one disruption, you're gone."

"Deal!" I quickly replied. I donned the hospital attire and moved to Dad's bedside. The large clock over the bed read 10 am.

My heart sank at the sight of my father. His wrists were tied to the bed, and were black from the bruising of his struggles. He was unconscious but moaning and writhing. I glanced at the heart monitor; it was a disaster! His heart would miss a beat or two, and then bunch several feeble beats together. He looked to be very near death.

140

A strange, aggressive anger welled up in me against what was happening too my dad. I laid my hands on him and rebuked the condition called death that held him in its cold grasp. I cursed that dark power in Jesus' name and commanded it to withdraw. Then I asked the Lord to flow into that feeble body with life and strength and healing.

It seemed I had just begun praying when the team of nurses returned to check and chart Dad's condition. Each time the nurses came, I stepped aside; when they left, I resumed my position of hands-on prayer.

Gradually Dad's moaning and writhing subsided. The pallor left his face; his breathing steadily became more normal. At about 10:30, I began to pray steadily in the prayer language that comes from the Holy Spirit. At 10:45, I checked the heart monitor; Praise God, it was recording the beat of a normal heart!

Just before 11 o-clock, Dad opened his eyes. "I knew you'd come," he said quietly.

"How do you feel, Dad?" I asked.

"I feel pretty good," he replied. "I have no pain and I feel a great peace. It's like I've been away somewhere, but I'm back, now."

"Yeah," I said, "Praise God, you're back!" I untied his wrists.

"Y'know," he said, "I could sure go a good cup of tea right now."

The nurse was passing by at that moment. "This man wants a cup of tea," I called out.

"What?" she said, in surprise. Then she asked Dad how he was feeling.

"I'm a little tired but I feel pretty good," said Dad.

I interrupted, "Well, can the man have his tea?"

She looked at me with that same steady gaze, "You damn right he can, even if I have to make it myself!" she said.

The nurses were back to check. "Look at this man, look at this chart, look at that monitor," their leader, said. "Since 10 o-clock, there has been progressive improvement in this patient's condition. This is amazing!" Nothing further was said, but she was fully aware that at 10 am, I began to pray for my dad.

Dad had tea and we visited, a lot. He steadily gained strength and was soon sitting up. They prepared to move him to a regular ward.

About that time, a seriously injured man in was brought in. His wife was, distraught and weeping. I nodded to the nurse in charge. "Is it okay if I go over there?" I asked. "Perhaps I can help."

"Yes," she replied, "I think you should go over there. Maybe you can help, I'm not sure we can."

I knelt beside the man's tearful wife and helped her to put her trust in Jesus. Then, together, we laid hands on her husband in Jesus' name. The Lord touched him and helped him remarkably.

Dad was leaving ICU and it was time for me to go. I thanked the young nurse for caring for Dad.

"No," she said, "I rather want to thank you for what you've done here today, Reverend," she said. "And any time you want to stop by again, it'll be fine with me."

CHAPTER 32

HOMER AND ETHEL

Homer Johnson was peeved. He had just turned 71 that fall, and the sawmill company laid him off.

As a new pastor in town, I was systematically going door to door, introducing myself in the community. On the north side of town, I came to a small house with a couple of big spruce trees in the front yard. I knocked, presently a small, gray-haired woman with lively blue eyes opened the door.

I introduced myself. She seemed friendly and said her name was Ethel Johnson. "Homer and I are just going to have tea; would you like to join us?" she asked.

"I'd like that," I assured her.

Homer Johnson sat at the kitchen table, a ruddy-faced outdoor type. We shook hands. He had the iron grip of a man who has worked with his hands for a lifetime. He gripped my hand with a lot more force than necessary. I matched him, and then some…Homer grinned. "You're a strong man for a preacher," he said.

"I've done other things besides preaching," I replied.

"Sit down, have some tea and tell us about it," said Homer.

"Well," I explained, "I was raised in the north, worked on the farm, ran a trapline, worked in the bush and in the sawmills. I boxed for a few years, worked in factories out east and was a commercial artist. Now I'm working for Jesus."

"How's the pay?" he asked.

"Out of this world!" I quipped.

Johnson laughed heartily. "Well, Reverend," he said, "we ain't had nothin' to do with church. Ain't had the time, ain't had the need."

"Everybody needs God," I countered. "You're going to stand before Him one day. Are you ready for that?"

The man reflected for a moment. "Ready as the next guy, I suppose," he finally responded, "I never really thought much about it."

"Homer," Ethel interjected, "now that you're not working at the mill we have more time. Maybe we should try going to church sometime."

Her husband did not seem convinced. He turned to me. "How did you get involved in this religion stuff anyway, Reverend?" He asked.

I shared the personal account of how Jesus had come into my life and transformed it in a miraculous way. As I spoke, I could see that the Holy Spirit was touching the hearts of that special couple.

"Man," said Homer, "that's quite a story! Does Jesus do stuff like that for just anybody?"

"He does," I assured him, "for any one who will surrender and believe." We talked some more, and then it was time for me to leave.

"Well come back and see us," said Ethel.

"Yeah," Homer added, "let's talk some more. Our door is open for you anytime."

I was happy to take them up on their invitation. We visited a number of times over the next few months, and we talked a lot about Jesus. One afternoon the three of us knelt before the living room sofa and Homer and Ethel Johnson gave their hearts to the Lord Jesus.

I had never asked them to church, but now they were both eager to attend.

"You're going to have to give us some instruction, Lee," Homer said, "We don't know how to behave in church, we've never gone before."

"Don't worry," I assured them, "the Lord loves you, and the people are friendly, you'll fit in just fine."

True enough, the congregation welcomed the Johnsons warmly, and the new couple felt right at home from the first Sunday.

On about their third Sunday morning, when I was half way through, what I thought was a pretty good sermon, I asked a rhetorical question. "What does this mean?" I thundered.

I noticed Homer glance around the room, then to my surprise he rose to his feet, and in answer to my question, he drawled, "Well Lee, I'll be damned if I know. What does that mean?"

There was a rash of clearing of throats and of coughing behind the hand, followed by a ripple of semi-controlled tittering, finally there was no holding back; the place erupted in waves of hearty belly laughs!

How do you recover a meeting when it's gotten out of control to this stage? I don't know.

Anyway, in time, the merriment subsided, and the sanctuary came to some sort of order. Only Homer and I were standing. Apparently, he was waiting for an answer.

"Well Homer,' I said, "I'll tell you what. If you'll let me finish up here, after the service we'll talk and I'll try and explain it."

"Okay," he replied, "good idea." He sat down and I tried to make sense of the rest of the message. I don't remember what I said, but it didn't matter much, I don't think anyone else remembered either.

One Sunday the Johnsons did not show up for church. I called later in the week to see if they were okay.

Ethel answered. "Well Pastor," she said, "we're having some trouble. Maybe you should come over and help us."

I hustled right over to their place. As soon as I stepped inside, I could feel the tension. The two were sour-faced.

Before I even got sitting down, Homer burst out, "Dammit Lee, Ethel cut me off! I've been sleeping on the couch for the last three nights!"

"You can't hang around the beer parlor till closing time, and then come home with a snoot-full," Ethel snapped, her blue eyes flashing, "I won't put up with it!"

"Whoa! Whoa!" I cautioned, holding up my hands. "You people are children of God, now. You are new creatures. Everything is different. You can solve your problems differently now than you ever could before."

"Yeah, how is that?" Homer queried.

"You can pray and have the Lord's help," I replied. "You can pray for each other, you can forgive each other, you can look in the Bible and see what the Lord has to say about it."

"Well," said Ethel, "what does the Lord have to say about a man who goes out drinking with his friends all night?"

"Listen to this," I returned, and read a few passages about the inadvisability of imbibing. Homer didn't like it, but he said nothing. His wife looked a little smug.

"You know, the Lord has said a few things about the marriage bed, too," I continued. I then read from 1 Corinthians 7, regarding the sexual responsibility of marriage partners to each other. Ethel was very uncomfortable with this.

"Is that how Jesus feels about these things?" Homer asked.

"Yeah, pretty much," I responded.

"Oh, Homer," Ethel said "we've both been wrong."

"Yeah, I know it," her husband replied.

"Let's pray now," I suggested, "we'll ask the Lord to help you both make things right with each other, and with Him." They both agreed so I prayed briefly.

"I think, with the Lord's help you folks can handle this now, don't you?" I asked.

"Yeah, I know what I've got to do," Homer said quietly.

"Me, too," his wife agreed.

The next Sunday the Johnsons came to church earlier than usual. They were smiling and at ease. Obviously, things were right again in the little house on the north side.

One day Ethel mentioned that their fiftieth Wedding Anniversary was coming up the following week. I congratulated them and enquired if a celebration was planned. They said no, the kids would not be coming home and they weren't doing anything special.

I shared this with my wife and the women at church. I wondered if we could organize an appropriate party for the new parishioners. The idea took fire, and the folks at the church outdid themselves in arranging a full-fledged banquet, on short notice. The lower auditorium was beautifully decorated. A head table was set up, complete with a huge anniversary cake.

The whole church family attended. Even the mayor stopped by and gave a congratulatory speech.

Months before, I had scheduled a series of meetings with Evangelist Ron Pierce, which were to commence that Sunday. Ron, also a much-loved gospel singer, arrived in time for the festivities. He sang a few pieces.

A reporter and photographer from the local newspaper also attended, and on the front page of the next week's paper was a beautifully written feature about the Anniversary Celebration, complete with photos. The couple was completely overwhelmed!

"We never had such a fuss made over us, even on the day we were married!" said Homer.

Later, he confided, "I'm off the beer, now, Lee"

"I'm glad to hear that, Homer," I responded, "How did it come about?"

"Well, heck, they ain't making it like they used to," he said. "It just ain't got the taste."

CHAPTER 33

THE SECOND TOUCH

Howard, a board member, dropped in at my office in the church one day. We chatted briefly, and then he said, "My father-in-law, Ewald, is in the hospital. Many of us have talked to him about the things of God, over the years, but he has never seen his need of a Savior. Audrey and I are wondering if you would talk to him."

"Be glad to," I replied, "I'll pay him a visit this afternoon."

About three o-clock I stopped at the hospital and called on Audrey's father, Ewald. He was a small man, quite soft-spoken. I could see, however, that he also possessed a resolute will.

We talked about many things, the farm, his experiences in the early days, and the lousy harvest weather. After a while I said, "Ewald, you sure must have done something right. You have a beautiful family, your wife and your children are Christians, they all serve the Lord." Then I asked him outright, "What about you, Ewald, what do you think about Jesus?"

The man had a few things to get off his chest. I let him get it all said. Then I had to agree with him that some, so-called Christians live disgusting lives, and some churches have gotten badly off-track. I went back to talking about Jesus, and presented the gospel in simple terms.

Beads of sweat began to appear on Ewald's upper lip. He wiped his palms on the hospital-issue robe he was wearing. I could tell that piece-by-piece, the Holy Spirit was dismantling a lifetime-worth of very stout walls in this man's inner life.

At last I said, "Don't you think its time this struggle came to an end and you just gave your heart to Jesus?"

He dropped his head and sort of slumped for a moment. Then he straightened up, took a deep breath and looked me in the eye. "You're right," he said firmly, "It is time I gave my heart to Jesus."

It was a joy to help him pray. And the faithful Jesus bore witness wonderfully of the miracle that had been granted. Before the supper hour, the whole family knew, and they rejoiced, too.

None of us expected the blow that came late that night. Ewald suffered a massive stroke. The prognosis for any recovery at all was dismal, at best. The family's joy turned to grave concern and heaviness of heart.

I went to the hospital as soon as I heard the bad news. Ewald lay unresponsive. His breathing was very deep, with the steady, almost mechanical rhythm that is often characteristic of stroke victims who are in a coma. I prayed, but there was no perceptible change.

I was deeply burdened for this man, who had so recently received Christ into his life. I was troubled also because this just did not seem to be God's way. I alerted many in the church to pray, and decided to spend the day in fasting and prayer, myself.

Late that evening, while in prayer at the church, an amazing sense of the presence of God filled the office. It seemed like all the burden and heaviness lifted in an instant. I felt a joyous relief, deep in the heart of my spirit. I sensed a silent voice speak there, "Be at peace, your prayers have been heard."

Well, I was at peace! I felt so right, so relaxed, I could not pray any more, it was over! I looked at my watch; it was twenty past ten.

I went home, had a light lunch, a good evening and a peaceful night.

About eight thirty the next morning I drove to the hospital and found Ewald, fully dressed and finishing off a breakfast of bacon and eggs!

There was more than a little excitement in the hospital that morning. Howard and Audrey were there. "Say," I said to them, "what were you doing at twenty past ten last night?"

"We were sitting right there beside the bed," Howard replied, "talking a little from time to time, but mostly just quietly praying. At one point, Ewald stopped breathing, then he took a deep breath, he turned over and began to breathe normally. For some reason, I looked at the clock there on the wall; it was twenty past ten. The nurses said he was out of the coma and was simply asleep. He slept peacefully all night, but at six-thirty this morning, he awoke, got up, and said he could eat a horse. He wondered when they were going to serve breakfast. They have given him a whole battery of tests already and can't find a thing wrong. Now he's raring to go home," Howard said.

"Praise the Lord!" I exclaimed. "This man isn't satisfied with one tremendous miracle, he's already had two! What's coming next?"

CHAPTER 34

NEVER TOO LATE

The town was small but our church was vibrant and active. Once a month it was our turn to host a service at the Senior's Hostel. Usually about a dozen people from the congregation accompanied me to the meeting. They helped with the music and singing and mingled with the residents.

For several months I noticed a very frail, old man in a wheelchair; he always arrived at the service a little late, and left just before the meeting wrapped up. Hmm, I thought, this man is hungry for God but there is something he does not want to face. I really wanted to talk to him, so at the next meeting, I asked one of the deacons to lead in the first couple of hymns. When the old man in the wheelchair arrived, late as usual, I strolled over and introduced myself.

He said his name was Fred, and that he had just turned 84. I said I would like to get to know him better and wondered if I could visit him sometime.

He was thoughtful before he answered. "Yeah, come in at three on Tuesday," he said, "They serve snacks at three, we can have coffee and talk some."

I showed up at three, Tuesday. Fred and I had coffee and got to know each other better. He was a farmer most of his life, and worked in the bush some. I could see by his frame and his large, bony hands that he had been a big, powerful man in his day. "I was six-five, and two-forty," he admitted.

"I'm glad you come out to the meetings, Fred," I said.

"Yeah, well, it's something to do, and the music is always good when your church comes," he replied with a shrug.

"What about Jesus?" I asked, directly.

He stiffened and turned his head away quickly. After a long silence, he took a deep breath and said, "I wonder if we could go up to my room and talk."

Fred's room was small and sparsely furnished. There was a bed, one chair and a table with a radio, a clock and several newspapers on it. A calendar from the local hardware adorned one wall.

I sat on the chair and left it up to Fred to open the conversation. I could see he was wrestling with things he wanted to say. Slowly, and with great effort he began, "I never cared a damn about God or church or nothing like that all my life. All I ever did was work. For some reason, I got to drinkin' a lot," he continued, "and when I drank I got mad at people. I beat up men in the beer parlor, I beat my wife, I beat my kids; I even whipped my horses, for God's sake!" Tears were streaming down his leathery cheeks, now. He was distressed and trembling. "I hated the way my dad treated me," he went on, "but it seemed like I couldn't help treating my own family the same way. My wife took the boys and left me years ago. I'm sure they all hate me, and I don't blame them a damn bit."

My heart went out to this broken, old man who was finally facing the truth about the failure of his life.

"To tell the truth," Fred resumed, "I never knew or cared if there was a God, until just lately. But you keep saying Jesus is real, and He's alive, and He's right here."

"That's true," I agreed.

"But even if it is true," he said, with a deep sadness in his voice, "it's too late now, anyhow, He wouldn't have anything to do with a man like me."

"Fred," I said, "it's for men like you that Jesus came to this earth. It's for men like you that He died." As I shared the simple truth of the gospel, the Spirit was overcoming darkness with light that day.

"You almost got me convinced," he said.

"It's not up to me to prove Jesus is real," I explained. "He'll do that Himself."

He seemed surprised. "What do you mean?" He queried.

"If you're ready to ask Jesus into your heart as your Savior and your Lord," I said, "the Spirit of Christ will come into your heart, and He'll make Himself real to you, right here," I said, tapping a finger on his bony chest.

Fred was thoughtful again for a while. "I want to do it!" he said. "I don't deserve it, and I don't know how it can happen, but I want to do it!"

The man's prayer of repentance and faith was so simple, forthright and honest I almost felt ashamed for having overheard it. Fred shed many tears.

After he finished praying, Fred was silent and thoughtful again. Finally, he turned to me and began, "Y'know, Pastor, I didn't see anything, and I didn't hear anything, but I feel something, something different. I feel peace I never had before, and I have a light feeling, right here," he said, patting the center of his chest. "Is that...Him?" he asked, almost in a whisper.

I nodded.

"I don't feel mad anymore," he went on, "I feel good inside, y'know...happy."

Fred's wrinkled face broke into a grin that revealed a set of cheap, tobacco-stained dentures. To me, that was a beautiful smile. I guessed not a whole lot of folks had ever seen Fred Roush smile.

I stayed a while. We talked together. We laughed together. We prayed together. It was a wonderful afternoon!

The next time we held a service at the Hostel, Fred was already in the common room, eager to get started.

Fred only made it to two more of those services; he died that summer.

CHAPTER 35

A MINER MIRACLE

Career miners, who work underground are a special breed of men.

Ron was such a man. He was a good friend and served on the church board of our small assembly of believers in a Saskatchewan mining town.

Some years before, Ron had received a serious neck injury in a mine accident. The neck gradually healed but there were consequences. Ron's neck had very little flexibility. He could barely rotate his head to either side. Besides this, he suffered periodic, debilitating headaches that could only be relieved by electronically controlled chiropractic adjustments.

One evening at the weekly Bible study and prayer service, Ron mentioned that he sensed the onset of one of his dreaded headaches. He asked if we would pray for him.

That night the group of perhaps eight or ten gathered around and laid hands on the miner. As I began to lead in prayer, I felt a strange anger rise up in me against the affliction that was troubling our friend. I began to speak to the condition and to rebuke it as though it had a life and an intelligence of its own. In Jesus' name, I commanded it to leave Ron's body and take it's symptoms with it. Then I asked the Lord to flow through the hurting man, by His Holy Spirit, and to reconstruct, and to realign and to heal all of the injured area.

We all sensed the presence and power of the Lord, remarkably, as we prayed there. After the "amen," everyone stepped back expectantly. There was a collective sense of assurance among us that the Lord had heard and answered our prayers.

We waited, motionless, but the rugged miner made no response.

I looked in his eyes and said, "Ron, in Jesus' name, turn your head..." This man's neck had been almost totally immobilized for years. I was asking for the impossible.

Ron sat as one paralyzed for several minutes, then, slowly he began to turn his head to the right, all the way, until his chin was near his shoulder. Then, slowly he rotated his head forward, and to the left, all the way. He had recovered full range of movement!

At that point, Ron came alive! He wagged his head back and forth rapidly and vigorously. "I have no pain! My headache is gone!" he shouted. "I've been healed! Thank God, I have been healed! Look!" he exalted, "my neck is free! Totally free!"

We rejoiced that night. We shouted, and we praised God, but Ron outdid us all! No one can really appreciate freedom like a person who has been in bondage for long, hard years. It is wonderful to be free, and as Jesus said, *"Whom the Son sets free, he shall be free indeed!"*

CHAPTER 36

A LESSON IN LOVE

I met Pentecostal Evangelist, Ken Bombay many years ago. His ministry has blessed thousands over the years, especially in the matter of leading Christians into true spiritual worship and a closer walk with Jesus. I invited Reverend Bombay for special meetings at various churches I pastored. I appreciated his gracious spirit, his sensitivity to the Lord and his genuine sense of humor. My wife and I became friends with Ken and his wife.

He was aware that the Lord was healing people in our church. I mentioned that we ministered to the sick according to James 5:14 and 15, which instructs that if the sick are anointed with oil by church elders, they will be healed, because of the prayer of faith.

Ken disagreed. He said, "Undoubtedly folks are being healed, here, but not according to that Scripture. The reason I say that is that there are no elders in your church. Even you are not an elder, for you are not yet ordained."

"That can't be right." I retorted. "How, then are people being healed?"

"They are being healed because of the gift of healing in your ministry, or, at times simply in answer to prayer," he explained. "In New Testament terms, elders are pastors, or shepherds, who have been called and anointed by God, ordained by the leadership and accepted by the local congregation. Anyhow," he continued, "you'll soon be ordained, then you'll be an elder."

"I don't think I agree with all that," I responded off-handedly.

"You'll find out some day," Ken replied, with a grin.

A few years passed, I moved to a new pastorate and was heavily involved in leading the new congregation into the fall season. There was a problem; I was not well. Some mysterious malady was steadily sapping my vitality. Doctors did not seem to be able to pinpoint the cause. I was generally weak, had very troublesome dysentery, and strangely, my teeth were ultra-sensitive. If I opened my mouth, every tooth went into cold-shock, just as though I had a mouth full of ice water.

About this time, I discovered that Ken Bombay was conducting a series of special meetings in Yorkton. I desperately wanted to attend those services, hoping to have prayer for my health problems. I was so busy however, that it was Thursday evening, before my wife and I got to go. We took a troubled young woman from the church with us.

The meeting was wonderful! It was refreshing to sit under Bombay's ministry again. The crowd was large and there were many needs. Ken called me to help him pray for folks at the altar. The young woman we had brought to the service was delivered and greatly helped. The line-up of people needing help seemed endless. Time slipped away and late that night we were heading home but I was still in distress. There was no opportunity to receive prayer for myself.

On Friday morning, I sought the Lord, earnestly. "Jesus, please help me," I prayed, "there just doesn't seem to be time to get to another meeting, but I desperately need Your healing touch."

He answered immediately; it was the silent voice of the Holy Spirit speaking deep inside. This is the message, as clearly as I can remember it, "If you attend the meeting tonight, My servant will speak on healing. When he asks those who need prayer to come forward, I want you to be the first to respond. My servant will pray; I will heal you."

Wow! Am I hallucinating? I wondered. Then I thought, no, this is real. I will do what He says.

I went by myself that night. I had just been seated when Ken came to the microphone; he seemed embarrassed. "I have to apologize to you folks," he began, "I know I've been announcing all week that I would be speaking on the Baptism in the Holy Spirit tonight. It has been advertised in the newspaper and on radio. I just never do this," he continued, "but for some reason I am compelled to change my sermon. I can't explain it, but I feel certain the Lord is telling me to speak about healing tonight and to pray for the sick."

"Thank You, Jesus," I whispered, "its happening."

The message was powerful. The evangelist taught, not only about the power of Jesus to heal, but about His love and desire to do so. Finally, Ken issued the appeal for those needing healing to come forward. I was out of the pew like an Olympic sprinter. I sidestepped past folks whose need was probably far greater than mine, but I was determined not to offend the Lord, even in this. Soon a number of others had lined up across the front. Evangelist Bombay laid hands on each one and prayed. I know the Lord touched many that night.

When Ken came to me in the line-up, he asked, "What is it my brother?"

"I don't know," I muttered, "I just need to be healed."

Ken reached into his jacket pocket and brought out a small bottle of oil. As he dabbed some on my forehead, he said, "I anoint you with oil in the name of the Lord Jesus Christ." Then he laid hands on me and prayed.

As that oil touched my forehead, the memory of the discussion we had had several years before, flashed into my mind. "Oh Lord," I cried in my spirit, "forgive me for arguing with a person far more spiritual than I. Lord, I just need Your grace tonight, and I reach out to receive it."

Before long, I was on the road out of town. As the miles clocked by, one-by-one, every distressing symptom left me. Before I was halfway home, I was perfectly well!

I felt very humble before the Lord that night. Of course, I was chided about the elders and oil issue, but the real lesson I learned was about the unlimited love and kindness of Jesus. It was humbling to realize that He would change an entire service for just one person, and not a very worthy one at that.

I would like to encourage every person who happens to be reading these words right now. The same Jesus has the same love for you that He showed to me that night. Do not give up. Continue to trust. It might take a while, but He will make a way to meet your need, too.

CHAPTER 37

DANCING FOR JESUS

The Lord worked many miracles of salvation and healing in our church in eastern Saskatchewan.

After the sermon one Sunday morning, I asked the congregation if there were any special needs that required prayer.

A woman of 71, who was a charter member of the church, limped slowly to the front. She explained that because of arthritis in her knee she had been taking cortisone shots for eight years. She had developed such a tolerance that her doctor would no longer administer the drug. "I'm in such pain now," she said, "I don't know where to turn, nothing seems to help. Please pray for me."

"I certainly will," I replied, and asked the congregation to join their faith with mine as we sought God for the suffering parishioner.

As I laid a hand on the woman's shoulder, something strange began to happen. Instead of praying for her healing, I found myself speaking in a loud voice to the condition of arthritis in her body. "You spirit called arthritis," I shouted, "I command you in the name of Jesus Christ to leave this woman's body! Come out of these bones, these joints, and these tissues! Go!" I shouted. "And pain, leave this body now, in Jesus' name!"

The little woman twirled gracefully away and began to dance across the front of the church. With eyes closed and hands raised, she stepped to the choreography of another world. She seemed to be laughing and crying at the same time and was obviously in tune with a spiritual dimension that was beyond the rest of us at the time.

We know that many churches have such joy and freedom in their times of praise and worship that dancing before the Lord is not uncommon. This, however, was not a dancing church. Moreover, that definitely was not a dancing woman. Truly, the Lord was doing a remarkable thing before our eyes!

As the dancer drew near, I put a hand gently on her shoulder. "Wait just a moment little lady," I said. Then I prayed, "Lord, I thank You for the wonder You are perform-ing here today. Now I ask that you would perfectly restore everything that has been damaged in this body. May she never be troubled by this condition again."

After a while, she came to the microphone and gave a testimony of what had happened. "Pastor," she said, "as soon as you spoke I could feel something release in my knee. And when you commanded it to leave–it went! Pain and all! I am pain-free, and my knee feels as though I had never, ever had arthritis.

Two years later, the little miracle woman and her husband paid us a visit in another city where I was then ministering. As we had tea and visited, I turned to her and asked, "What about the knee?"

She stomped her foot vigorously several times. "My knee is a hundred percent perfect!" she exclaimed, "Don't you know the Lord does all things well?"

CHAPTER 38

FAITH OVER THE LONG HAUL

Trust and faith are next of kin. They are related and similar but there are some differences, the chief difference being duration. Trust in God is really faith over the long haul. Faith can only grow and increase in value and power as it faces rugged testing and trial, and the test of time is often the toughest challenge of all.

I keenly remember a serious challenge that spanned a six-month period and stretched my faith to the limit. Ultimately, though, it affected my life in a profound and a lasting way.

I was the pastor of an eastern Saskatchewan church. Things were fairly predictable at the time, when seemingly, out of nowhere, the opportunity arose to purchase a car from an estate sale at an unusually low price. It was a deluxe model Chrysler in immaculate condition. The car was seven or eight years old, but an elderly person who seldom took it out of the garage had owned it. The mileage was extremely low. The interior even had that unmistakable new-car smell. I was ecstatic, when the deal was finally made. It was a beautiful car and I fully believed the Lord had a hand in making it mine, and I earnestly praised Him for it.

One morning several months later, I was astonished to discover my new car was gone! I called the RCMP; they informed me that they had located my car on the Trans-Canada Highway, and had it at the Police garage in Indian

Head. Forensics was checking it for fingerprints, so I arranged for a time that I could pick it up.

The next day a friend drove me to Indian Head. I was devastated to learn that because of extensive damage, my Chrysler was a write-off; I never drove it again.

Back at my office, it was time to get on my knees before the Lord and find some answers and some direction. "Lord, where were Your angels?" I cried. "What happened to Your hand of protection? Have I offended You in some way? How could this happen? And why?"

The heavens were as brass, and I received no clear response from the Lord. At last, though feeling discouraged, I felt I should just make the best decision I could and move on.

The payout from the insurance company was prompt but paltry. They paid on a scale in accordance with the age of the vehicle, which left me with a check for $600, not much to go car shopping with.

I had to have a car quickly so I bought one off a local lot for a little more than my six hundred. It was a Chrysler, several years newer than the one that was stolen, but not half the car. The suspension needed work and it did not handle well. The paint was starting to peel and the interior was downright scruffy. It had squeaks and rattles and sometimes it was hard to start. Every time I sat behind the wheel of that junker, I thought of the other car. A kind of a sadness settled over my spirit. I struggled against it and prayed a lot; but it was just there.

I received an invitation to pastor a new church in a city farther south. I accepted the call. The move would be in July. The men who would have helped me move to the new location would be on holiday, so I volunteered to look after the move myself. The new congregation was to reimburse me later.

I borrowed a truck from a friend on moving day, and made the trip alone.

It was a hot summer's day, but there were some strange clouds forming in the west. About forty miles east of

Regina I spotted a small funnel-cloud, a little prairie twister dancing across a wheat field off to the north. It veered and came toward the highway. I tried to miss it by altering speed, but as though it were laser-guided, that twister hit the truck dead-on! There was a sharp impact; the truck lurched left, then right. I glanced in the rear-view mirror to see more than half our family's belongings being vacuumed out of the back of that truck, and strewn across the highway! I saw a leather-covered chair I had inherited from my late father, sail fifteen feet into the air and crash to the pavement.

The twister was gone in a moment, but now a hard-driving rain raked the countryside. I was out of the truck immediately, retrieving everything I could. Much of it was just gone. Many things were broken. I could see some of my wife's music being scattered across a field. Some of my young son, Danny's things were smashed to bits there on the highway.

There was quite a bit of traffic, but nobody stopped. That seemed callous to me. Could they not see I was a man in trouble, battling wind and rain out on the highway, trying to recover his family's possessions?

At one point, I was on my hands and knees gathering up some of Danny's toys, when a car whipped past and crushed them before my face!

That's what really broke me. I turned away from it all, got into the truck and slammed the door.

I could not stop crying for a long time. Then I had it out with the Lord. I said, "Lord, those years ago You saved me and I praise You for it. I gave you my heart and my life and I meant it. Now You've put me into the ministry. But, Lord," I continued, "I'm not the only one paying the price. My wife and children have had to give up everything, too, so that I could serve You. They have left a new house, and friends they love, so we could be here. We don't have much, Lord, but there it is, all smashed up on the highway. Is that it, Lord?' I cried, "Is that all it matters to You?"

I said many other things. Things I should never have said, things I did not really mean.

After a while everything was quiet. The rain had stopped, the wind had blown itself out and the prairie sun was comforting the ruffled wheat fields once again.

In the quietness of the truck cab, the Lord began to speak into my spirit. He assured me that He loved me, and He made me understand that He knew everything that had happened, and that He felt it all. He urged me to always trust, because, whether I could sense it or not He would always be with me, I should therefore always trust.

As I slipped the truck into gear and proceeded west, though I had a peace in my heart that had been missing for months, I was still heavyhearted about the fact that I had yet to look my wife and my boy in the face and tell them that many of their things were lost and broken out on the highway, and I could not save them.

In the months that followed, we worked hard at fitting into the new congregation and the new community. Things were going well in both areas, but as fall gave way to another prairie winter, the shortcomings in the car we drove became increasingly apparent. The well-worn motor struggled to perform, and on the coldest mornings sometimes, it just would not start. In addition, the heater was woefully inefficient. I had gotten past my earlier negativity about the car, but it definitely was not the joy of my life, and I longed for the day we could afford a better one.

Throughout my years in the ministry, I have generally kept Monday as a day off. I tended to put everything into meeting the demands of the weekend and needed the day after to relax and recuperate. If there was a day to sleep later in the morning and be at ease, it was always Monday.

One Monday morning later in that first winter, the phone rang. A cheerful voice asked, "Is this Pastor Updike?"

"It is," I replied.

"This is Darlene from Saskatchewan Government Insurance," the voice chirped on, "I wonder if you could come to our downtown office this morning. We have a car for you."

"That's very nice," I responded patiently, "You've certainly made my day!" I prepared to hang up, thinking it was some kind of a joke.

"Oh, no, no," the voice said, "don't hang up, this is really true. There really is a car here for you. All you have to do is sign a couple of documents and it's yours."

"That's preposterous!" I retorted.

"No, it's wonderful!" the chirpie voice declared. "I've never seen anything like this before. Why don't you come right down and see for yourself?"

"Yeah, well...okay, okay," I muttered, "I'll come down."

I said to Bev, "That was SGI; they want me to come down to the office, something about a car for me."

"What do they mean?" my wife asked.

"Beats me," I said with a shrug, "You'd better come along, just in case there's actually something to this."

When we walked into the SGI office that morning, everything stopped. All of the office employees gathered around the front desk as we approached.

"Reverend Updike?" a young woman asked.

I recognized the voice from the phone. I nodded, and glanced around at the circle of onlookers. They seemed excited, as though they were part of something very special. I was starting to wonder...

Darlene slid several documents across the counter. "These are the registration and insurance," she explained. "Just sign where the x's are."

"Wait a minute, hold on!" I broke in, "Someone has bought a car for me? Where is the purchaser's name?" I scanned the pages but the purchaser's name was blacked out. I noticed that the vehicle described was a late model Chrysler. "Who has done this?" I demanded.

"You'll never find out from us!" Darlene affirmed. I observed that the crowd of witnesses were all nodding in agreement, and grinning from ear to ear as well.

"Look Reverend," Darlene continued cheerfully, "some folks think you should be driving a whole lot better

166

car than you're driving. My advice is, sign these papers, take your car and enjoy it. And don't spend a lot of time trying to find out where it came from, how about it?"

She handed me a pen and spread the papers before me again.

"Okay…okay," I stammered, "I guess that's the thing to do." I signed the documents and passed them back across the counter.

"Thank you, Reverend," said Darlene, "and here are your keys." She dropped two sets of keys into my hand, and, leaning forward, she pointed out the front window, "and there, is your car!"

I could not believe it; there sat a Chrysler Newport Custom Sedan. Its polished exterior glistened in the early morning sunlight. What a beauty! It was not brand new, but it was late model, and everything about it was pristine. I found out years later, by accident, that it had been the personal vehicle of the city's Chrysler dealer himself, and that he had spared nothing to keep it 'show-room'.

Bev drove the old car home, and I slid behind the wheel of that special car. Everything about it was perfect.

I am sure you can understand that before I had traveled a block and a half I had to pull over, and just thank the Lord. I asked Him to pour out His mighty blessing on those unknown people who had done such a gracious thing. However, I also remembered that summer afternoon in the cab of the truck. The message was to always trust. He is always with you whether you can sense it or not, so–always trust.

CHAPTER 39

RUNNING DUMB

In mid-summer on the southern Saskatchewan prairie, two weather conditions are normal; it is going to be hot! And it is going to be windy!

Some years ago, I lived in the city of Weyburn. In those days, I was a daily runner. I ran ten miles several times a week, and shorter distances on other days. I was not a jogger, I ran hard.

I embarked on a ten-mile run one very hot Saturday afternoon. The route followed a little-used highway north of the city. The road surface was paved, but the shoulders were gravel. I ran on the left side, facing traffic. If a vehicle approached, I simply stepped to the left onto the graveled shoulder and kept running until the pavement was clear again. I ran five miles out and five miles back.

I had not checked the day's temperature but before I had gone a mile, I knew this was one blistering hot day! The oppressive heat seemed to siphon away vitality with every stride. I considered it just another challenge, however, and drove myself to maintain my usual pace.

At mile four, I was really struggling, and actually not feeling too well. There had been almost no traffic, but a red Camaro coming out of the city overtook me, slowed to match my pace and pulled over into the southbound lane beside me. The driver, a baldish man of about 40, rolled down the window and thrust a litre-sized soft drink out at me. "Here, drink," he said.

I grunted thanks, grabbed the plastic cup and gulped through the straw. I kept stride while the red car idled along beside me.

"Drink more," the driver encouraged, "you're going to need it."

I was glad to comply. That drink seemed like a magic elixir of some kind, it provided a jolt of almost instantaneous revitalization. I imagined I could feel the cool fluid coursing through my veins.

"Take another good shot," the bald man said, "Don't be afraid, you won't overdo it, and you need the fluid."

I took another generous swig and handed the cup back.

"How far you going?" the man asked.

"Ten," I panted, "The next intersection is my turn-around point."

"Look," the guy in the Camaro said, "this is the hot-test day we've had in years, it's 104 degrees out here! It's too damn hot to even jog, much less to run hard like you're doing. Furthermore, don't ever run this kind of distance in summer, without taking water. You're lucky you haven't keeled over from heat exhaustion." The man went on to give me a thorough dressing-down about 'running dumb' as he called it. Then he grinned and shoved the cup out to me, again. "Here, load up," he said, "You've got a long way to go."

I took another hefty drink and handed the cup back. "Thanks," I mumbled, nodding toward the cup. "And thanks for your…ah, advice."

"Sure," he replied, "and you pay attention to what I've said. And slow down on the way back."

I nodded.

The guy floored the Camaro and in a few minutes, it was just a red speck on the prairie highway.

I came to the five-mile intersection, crossed the highway and headed back for town. I slowed to an easy jog. I was still stinging a little from the tongue-lashing, but then I turned to the Lord and wondered if He had something to say in all of this.

My mind was bombarded with thoughts as I traveled those last five miles. I am sure some of them had their origin in the Holy Spirit.

Of course, it was foolhardy to be running hard, for that distance, in that heat, with no water.

Even in our folly though, Jesus does not turn away from us; He sent a guy in a red Camaro, with a big, cold drink in his hand. He sent a guy a guy who knew running; a guy with common sense who was not afraid to talk straight about it.

Life however, is not just about running out on the road. Yet how many times in some of the serious issues of life have we made a major decision without first praying it through? Or taken some new direction without fully weighing the consequences?

Life is like a race set before us. The course is uniquely designed by Jesus to fit each of us perfectly. We are to run with our eyes on Him; looking for His guidance, trusting in His power. I was reminded that day, that the race we are running is a pathway toward maturity. We are growing up in Jesus. 'Running dumb' just doesn't cut it!

CHAPTER 40

MANS' BEST FRIENDS

Some folks have a way with dogs; it is amazing to watch. It is as though an instant friendship is established between human and animal, though they may have never met. I cannot say that I have been a dog-lover. I don't hate them mind you, but I just do not have the ease with dogs that some have.

I owned a dog when I was a boy on the farm; he was a remarkable animal and a wonderful friend. After Shorty's death, I really didn't have too much to do with dogs. Perhaps sub-consciously, I just didn't want to chance facing the pain of losing another such friend. None of this has hindered the Lord from using dogs to teach me some profound lessons, however.

On a rainy Saturday afternoon in Saskatoon, one of the Lord's dog-lessons faced me head-on and without warning. It was early spring and stubborn patches of snow skulked in shaded areas. A cold drizzle had settled in for the day. The depressing grayness fit well my own demeanor at the time. A lot of negative factors had accumulated to bring a pall of discouragement, even with my spiritual life.

I was a daily runner in those times, of usually five or six miles. That Saturday I had only gone a few blocks when I noticed a large dog ahead, a German shepherd. Dogs and runners are often not a happy mix. Most dogs seem to feel uneasy when they see an adult running nearby. I have observed them become progressively more agitated and sometimes even attack. I hoped it would not be the case this day. As I drew nearer, the dog began barking in an unfriendly manner. There was nowhere else to go, so I decided to proceed carefully.

Now the animal began barking furiously and trotting toward me, stiff-legged, hackles raised; it did not look good. When I stepped off the curb, he left the sidewalk across the intersection and bounded toward me, barking and snarling viciously.

A multitude of thoughts raced through my mind in a fraction of a second. It seemed certain that I was going to go hand-to-hand with a shepherd; not exactly a comforting prospect. Having a history of some years in boxing and other dangerous pursuits, I felt I could somehow defend myself, but might possibly suffer some injury. I did not actually pray, but the thought came that if I was as close to the Lord as I once had been, He would help me.

No time for speculations now, we were running right at each other! I decided to let him commit himself and trust my instincts to react. At a distance of about ten feet, he swerved. The faint hope that he might be bluffing evaporated in a second; he whirled and came from the left flank.

I was flying now, running flat-out. He overtook me in a few bounds, and then with a snarl, he leaped for my throat!

Before I could react, a miracle that I can never forget played out before my eyes. An unseen power (whether an angel, or the Spirit of Christ Himself, I do not know) grabbed that dog in mid-air and twisted his head downward so that the back of his head hit me in the left hip. I heard his jaws snap together twice. Then the same force upended him and drove him face-first into the pavement like a pile driver!

The animal was stunned for a moment. I kept moving but slowly now, watching carefully. The shepherd revived quickly and leaped to his feet. He stared at me wide-eyed, appearing to be terror-stricken. Then, to my amazement, he cried like a small puppy, whirled and ran the other way! He continued to cry like a pup that had its tail caught in a door, looking repeatedly over his shoulder as he ran away from me at top speed. I could still hear him yelping long after he had turned the corner a block down the street.

I was flabbergasted...dumbfounded...this sort of thing does not happen in the real world...does it? I don't know just what happened out there on the street. All I know for sure is that somehow, it was Jesus. A sense of the presence of God settled over me there in an almost overwhelming way. Tears poured from my eyes and mingled with the rain running down my face. Finally, I prayed, out loud, "Lord, why did you do this?"

There was nothing for a moment, and then a voice spoke. Not an audible voice, but a soft, kind voice spoke these words in the heart of my spirit, "Because I love you."

I could hardly bear it; the force of that revelation was so strong. He loves me, personally, as an individual. He did all of this–for me, and I had not even asked for His help.

I have been different since that day.

I know the Lord has that same personal, intimate love for every human being. Unfortunately, the circumstances of life, the treacherous work of the devil, and our own hang-ups often combine to distort our view of Jesus. I say, "Lord, help us all to see You as You really are!"

A very different experience concerning dogs happened to me many years later in the city of Edmonton. I had given up running in favor of a brisk daily walk. It was a crisp winter morning, and I was walking east on 129B Avenue. Suddenly two huge dogs were running toward me at high speed. One was black and quite a bit larger than the average German shepherd. The other was of equal size but had long white hair.

I knew instantly that if these dogs were bent on attacking, my chances were not good since I am now a senior, and these were two very large dogs. I spoke, but quietly, "Lord, I trust You in this."

The two raced toward me as one. I continued walking. When they were almost upon me they stopped, separated, turned and fell into step beside me, the black on my left, and the white on the right. We made no eye contact. In fact, they did not pay me much attention at all. They behaved as though they were on a mission and were under orders. The two animals matched me stride-for-stride, their large bodies occasionally brushed against my legs. I prayed, "Lord, I don't understand this, but so far, so good."

The two dogs behaved like personal bodyguards. They remained disciplined and very alert, as though keeping the surroundings under careful surveillance. Much like secret service agents guarding a president. Everyone we met gave us a very wide berth, even stepping out into the street to let us pass. I noticed a few were annoyed; obviously thinking, the old guy should keep his monstrous dogs on leash. I actually started to relax and even enjoy it a little. I felt the two furry companions were protecting me; though I was not aware of any danger.

By now, we had turned north on 91st Street. Halfway up the second block a German shepherd guarded the back-yard of a big brick house. Each day that I passed that way, he was at the chain-link fence making a lot of threatening noise. This day he rushed to the fence, barking as usual. Immediately the two dogs with me faced him down. They made no sound, but in a moment, the barking stopped and I saw the shepherd slink into his kennel.

The two resumed their position, black on the left, white on the right, and the three of us commanded the sidewalk as we headed up to 132nd Avenue. Here I turned west. Several blocks on, just past the elementary school, the dogs became alarmed at something suspicious to them at a house across the street. Side by side, they loped through the morning traffic to investigate. I wondered if they would be back, and quickened my pace.

In a few minutes they bounded swiftly back across the busy street and once again we walked on, three abreast, black on the left, white on the right, old guy in the middle.

As we approached my residence on 95A Street I slowed down, they slowed, too. Finally, I stopped and spoke to the pair for the first time, "This is as far as I go," I said.

They ignored me and crossed the street. Then, in unison, they stopped, turned and looked fully at me for the first time. We stood for a full minute looking at each other. "Thanks," I said.

They looked at me for perhaps another 30 seconds, then turned and trotted purposefully on toward 97th Street.

I have prayed and pondered about these strange dog experiences, considerably. It is unwise to spiritualize everything that happens, trying to assign significance where perhaps there is none. (Christianity, we know, is not mysticism.) Nevertheless, with Jesus, nothing is random and there are no accidents.

With the first experience of being attacked while running, there came a great revelation of the love of God. I already knew of His power; through this experience, I came to understand His love much more clearly.

In the second experience of being escorted by the two large dogs, there came a new awareness that the Lord is watching over me. My safety and protection are out of my hands, they are in His. I have seen Psalm 23:6 in a different light ever since that day. *"Surely Goodness and Mercy shall follow me all the days of my life."*

I do not know what the names of those two dogs are, but to me, the black is 'Goodness,' and the white is 'Mercy.'

CHAPTER 41

THE COMING OF THE LORD

Blair and Ethel were an important part of our church family. Both in their eighties, they were down to earth folks who knew spiritual reality.

Ethel had struggled with cancer for some time, and though she was not suffering a great deal of pain, she was in a weakened condition.

One afternoon as I visited her in the hospital, she seemed troubled and said she had a question to ask. Apparently, Ethel had never been baptized in water. Her family had moved a lot in her early life and later, mostly through neglect she said, she just had not pursued it.

I believe she sensed her life was nearing its conclusion, and she wondered how to face the Lord with what she now considered a major disobedience.

"Pastor, what can be done?" she asked, "I believe immersion is the correct mode of baptism, but I am too weak to even leave the hospital now. How can I be baptized?"

"Water baptism is important," I replied, "however, not everyone has a chance to experience it. The thief on the cross for instance was not baptized, yet Jesus assured him a place in paradise."

"Yes," she responded, "but I had lots of chances; I just didn't see that it was done."

"Ethel," I said, "Jesus has forgiven you of so many things, do you not think He will forgive you for this misdemeanor, also? And here is something else to consider," I went on, "the modes of baptism are merely symbols. Perhaps immersion is more correct. Remember though, sprinkling is a useable symbol, too. If you would feel better about it, I will go to the kitchen right now, get a pitcher of water, and baptize you. I am sure the Lord will accept it.

Ethel closed her eyes for a few minutes. Then she said, "No, Pastor, as you have said, the Lord has so graciously forgiven me of so much, I know He will forgive this, too."

A few days later Ethel's condition worsened drastically. I called at the hospital frequently.

On Wednesday, it was our church's turn to host the service at the Senior's Haven. On my way to the service, I stopped at the hospital to see how Ethel was. I enquired at the nurse's station. The nurse took me aside. "This woman is very close to death, Pastor Lee," she confided. "Her mind is clear but her body is shutting down."

I went to the room quickly. I found, as the nurse had said, Ethel's mind was surprisingly clear. Her countenance radiated a quiet peace.

"Pastor," she said, "I believe my time has come. Do you see that cloud over there in the corner of the room?"

"No, I don't see anything," I replied.

"It's all right," she said softly, "when you leave it will come back. For the last half hour, I have watched a beautiful cloud forming there in the corner. When anyone else comes into the room, it gradually fades. When they leave, it returns. I think it's a 'Jesus sign,' I believe He is coming for me. Do you believe me?"

The presence of Jesus was very discernable in that room. I could see the peace of God on her face; I could hear it in her voice.

"Yes, Ethel," I answered, "I believe you."

It was time for the senior's service and I had to leave. "I'll come back right after the service," I promised. We said our good-bys before I left...just in case.

I hurried to the Senior's Haven and conducted the service. As soon as the meeting concluded, I rushed back to the hospital.

I approached the nurse's station quickly. The nurse looked solemn; she shook her head. "Gone?" I asked.

She nodded.

I have been encouraged many times, as I have thought about Ethel's deathbed vision. Certainly, I believe that one day the Lord Jesus will return to this earth and set up his literal Kingdom. However, in another very real sense, I believe that when a genuine believer leaves this life, it is Jesus who comes for him or her. PSALMS 116:15 says, *"Precious in the sight of the Lord is the death of His saints."* He will not be sending an angel, as they show us on TV. Moreover, it will not be Saint Peter. PSALMS 23:4, *"Even though I walk through the valley of the shadow of death, I will fear no evil, for You are with me..."* It is Jesus who will be there! ACTS 1:9-11 describes the ascension of Christ. It records that; *"a cloud received Him out of their sight."* An angel announced to the disciples that He would return the same way. I take that to mean, He will come from above, and there will be a cloud.

I have a strong feeling that the Lord Jesus stepped out of the cloud in the corner of that hospital room and welcomed His servant, Ethel into her eternal dwelling place.

AFTERWORD

Truly, God is a God of miracles and of wonders. The greatest of His wonders among human beings is the wonder of redemption, by which, an ungodly, degenerate sinner can be transformed into a holy and a godly person. This astonishing change is not wrought by human effort, but is freely bestowed by the grace of God, in response to repentance and faith.

Prayer is the connection between man and God, through which the gift of salvation is received. Untold millions have found peace with God by praying a simple prayer such as this–

"Lord Jesus, I realize today that I am a sinner. I repent of it and ask Your forgiveness. I believe Your blood was shed, You died on the cross for me, and that the Father has raised You from the dead. Jesus, I believe You are present with me and You hear me pray. Please come into my heart, make me a child of God and grant me the gift of eternal life. I receive You now as my Savior and my Lord. Please help me live, as You want me to. Amen."

If you have not yet received Jesus Christ into your heart and your life, may I repeat the question I asked at the conclusion of Chapter one–"Why not try God?"

Carefully examine this prayer. If it accurately expresses the desire of your heart, pray it in all sincerity. Believe that the Lord is present with you, and that He will grant everything you have asked.

Receiving Christ as Savior, is a powerful experience; spiritual growth and maturing however, is a lifetime process, perhaps an eternal one. To enable that process to succeed it is important that we get involved in a church where the love of God and spiritual reality abound, and where we can enjoy the benefit of fellowship with godly Christians. The Bible is mana for the soul; prayer, praise and worship are indispensable to the spirit, and sharing our faith pleases God, and blesses others. This is normal Christian living.

As the children of God on earth, we enjoy His wondrous blessings. Nevertheless, sometimes there are extreme challenges to our faith; the pressures and temptations of the world, the malevolent cunning of the devil, and the shallowness of our own human nature.

In addition, we Christians are not exempt from some of the hardship and loss that others endure. However, with us there is one enormous difference. We face everything following the guidance, and trusting the power of the Lord Jesus Christ! In the midst of trials, we rejoice and flourish!

ROMANS 8:37 *"Yet in all these things we are more than conquerors through Him who loved us."*

The Father's desire for us is that our Christian life should be interesting, exciting, and fulfilling. We are meant to walk in the love, the joy and the peace of God, and to know the reality of His presence and His power.

1CORINTHIANS 2:9 gives us an inkling of what our final destination will be like–*"Eye has not seen, nor ear heard, nor have entered into the heart of man the things which God has prepared for those who love Him."*

Heaven is beyond our wildest dreams! If we walk with Jesus in life here, this is how we will stand before Him on that day–JUDE 24-25 *"Now to Him who is able to keep you from falling, and to present you faultless before the presence of His glory with exceeding joy. To God our Savior, who alone is wise, be glory and majesty, dominion and power, both now and forever. Amen."*